VARIATIONS ON
A STARTER

JEAN CONIL and HUGH WILLIAMS

NEW ENGLISH LIBRARY/TIMES MIRROR

Also by Jean Conil and Hugh Williams and available from New English Library:
VARIATIONS ON A RECIPE

First published in Great Britain in 1980 by
Judy Piatkus (Publishers) Limited

First NEL Paperback Edition April 1981

NEL Books are published by
New English Library Limited,
Barnard's Inn, Holborn,
London EC1N 2JR.

Reproduced, printed and bound in Great Britain by
Cox & Wyman Ltd, Reading

0 450 05060 2

CONTENTS

EGGS and CHEESE

SOUPS

VEGETABLE STARTERS

INTRODUCTION

Variations on a Starter is the second volume in our successful series which began with *Variations on a Recipe*. The idea on which the series is based is a new and simple approach to cooking: by learning how to vary dishes you can get greater use and value out of recipe books, as well as becoming less dependent on them.

Each recipe in *Variations on a Starter* is given in detail and with each one you are shown how to make variations on it. So from the sixty basic dishes you can learn to make hundreds more, and you can select which variations suit your particular taste and budget.

The first volume in the series dealt with a wide range of different dishes, from soups and sauces to main courses and puddings. This book is about first courses — starters — which, in many cases can be expanded into a main course, or eaten as a snack.

We have divided the book into eight sections — each for a different type of starter. We deal with everything from pasta to egg and cheese starters, and include sections on pâtés, fruit, fish, vegetable, salad and soup starters.

The recipes in the book are either original dishes created by Master Chef Jean Conil, or else they are traditional dishes with exciting new variations. In this way, using the ideas we suggest, you should be able to build up your own confidence as a cook, so that in time you will be able to make variations to your own favourite dishes and even create original menus.

Each recipe, as in *Variations on a Recipe*, has been laid out to make reference as clear and easy as possible. Each one is given on a double page with ingredients and method followed by preparation and cooking time, portions and calories per portion, and finally the variations and chef's tips. These tips are little bits of advice that Jean Conil has collected, discovered or invented over the years, and can save a great deal of time, as well as improving your culinary technique.

A good cook is inventive and ingenious, able to make a delicious meal from anything that's in the larder. We hope this book will help you towards being a better cook. Use the book as a conventional recipe book by all means, but also try to create new and original dishes to suit yourself. Be adventurous, and make your cooking more fun.

Weights and Measurements

In listing the ingredients for each recipe, we have tried to make it as easy as possible for you to refer to when shopping and cooking. The ingredient is followed by the quantity in convenient measurements like teaspoons and cups, as well as in imperial and metric weights. Hence oil is listed like this: **Oil** 4 Tbs (2fl oz/50ml). The abbreviations "tsp" and "Tbs" are used for teaspoon and tablespoon respectively.

Since the introduction of metric measurements, recipes have had to include weights in both imperial (ounces and pounds) and metric (grams and millilitres) measurements. This poses a number of problems. The difficulty is in finding sensible equivalents; for example, one ounce is actually just over 28 grams. In the following table therefore you will see 1oz = 25-30g. In many instances it does not matter whether you use 25 or 28 or 30. But think carefully about the dish in question and the particular ingredient if you vary the quantity too much.

WEIGHT

Metric	Imperial	Metric	Imperial
15g	½oz	450g	16oz (1 lb)
20g	¾oz	900-1000g	2 lb (1 kg)
25-30g	1oz	1½ kg	3 lb
40g	1½oz	2 kg	4 lb
50g	2oz	2½ kg	5 lb
75g	3oz	3 kg	6 lb
100g	4oz(¼ lb)	3½ kg	7 lb
150g	5oz	4 kg	8 lb
175g	6oz		
200g	7oz		
225-240g	8oz(½ lb)		
250g	9oz (¼ kg)		
275g	10oz		
300g	11oz		
350g	12oz (¾ lb)		
375g	13oz		
400g	14oz		
425g	15oz		

VOLUME

Metric	Imperial	US Cup
50ml	2fl oz	¼
75ml	2½fl oz	$\frac{1}{3}$
	3fl oz	$\frac{3}{8}$
100ml	4fl oz	½
150ml	5fl oz (¼ pint)	$\frac{5}{8}$
200ml	6fl oz	¾
	7fl oz	$\frac{7}{8}$
225ml	8fl oz	1
275ml	9fl oz	$1\frac{1}{8}$
300ml	10fl oz (½ pint)	1¼
	11fl oz	$1\frac{3}{8}$
	12fl oz	1½
400ml	14fl oz	1¾
	16fl oz	2 = 1 pint (US)
½ litre (500-600ml)	20fl oz (1 pint)	
750ml (¾ litre)	1¼ pints	
900ml	1½ pints	
1 litre	1¾ pints	

Equivalent Oven Temperatures

°C	°F	Gas Mark
110	225	¼
130	250	½
140	275	1
150	300	2
170	325	3
180	350	4
190	375	5
200	400	6
220	425	7
230	450	8
240	475	9

SPOONS
(level unless otherwise stated)

Metric	Imperial
1.25ml	¼ tsp
2.5ml	½ tsp
5ml	1 tsp
15ml	1 Tbs
30ml	2 Tbs (1fl oz)
3 tsp	1 Tbs
2 Tbs	1fl oz
16 Tbs (US)	1 cup (US)

LINEAR MEASURE

Metric	Imperial
3mm	⅛in
5mm	¼in
1 cm	½in
2.5cm	1in
4cm	1½in
5cm	2in
6.5cm	2½in
7.5cm	3in
10cm	4in
12.5cm	5in
15cm	6in
18cm	7in
20cm	8in
23cm	9in
25cm	10in
30cm	12in(1 ft)
35cm	14in
38cm	15in
45cm	18in
60cm	24in
92cm	36in

BAR MEASURES

Dash	4-6 drops
Teaspoon	⅛fl oz
Tablespoon	½fl oz
Pony/liqueur glass	1fl oz
Jigger	1½fl oz
Wineglass	4fl oz
Cup	8fl oz

Physics and Chemistry

The best chefs and cooks don't need recipe books. They use well tried and tested formulae to make their creations. While we are not suggesting that you turn your ordinary kitchen into a chemistry laboratory, we are giving you certain guidelines that will help you to concoct your own dishes if you want to.

Some principles in creating a recipe are as follows:

Seasoning:
> Salt required is one per cent in weight of the total ingredients: e.g. 1 lb (450 grams) mashed potato needs 4.5 grams of salt (roughly one level teaspoon).

Spicing:
> 0.01 per cent of weight: e.g. 1 lb (450 grams) of minced meat needs a minimum of ½ gram pepper.

Wine in Sauce:
> A sauce containing wine should have no less than 40 per cent of the total amount of sauce as wine. But if you use fortified wines like port or sherry, reduce the amount of alcohol to 20 per cent.

Herbs:
> If you use fresh herbs you need ½oz (15 grams) per 1 lb (450 grams) of food. If you use the dried variety, cut the quantity to one eighth of an ounce or 4 grams per pound of food. **N.B.** Some herbs, like sage and thyme, are strong; perhaps add less.

Acidity:
> For a fish sauce you need acidity e.g. 2 Tbs white vinegar per pint of sauce (600mls) or the juice of one lemon.

Sweetening:
> Sugar content should be:
>
> For jams and jellies . . . . 66 per cent
> For jam sauce not more than . . . . 25 per cent
> In milk pudding not more than . . . . 15 per cent
> For cakes and sponges . . . . 25 per cent
> For light sponge . . . . 30-33 per cent
> In meringue . . . . 75 per cent

For light meringue .... 50 per cent
In caramel and hard sweets. .... 99 per cent
In sweet and sour sauces and chutneys........ 10 per cent

Balancing Cakes

● For a perfect cake you need a good patent flour. The calculation is based on the different quantities of eggs, fat, sugar and flour.
● A reduction in one liquid must be made up by another liquid.
● But if eggs are replaced by water, an aerating agent must be used with flour (Baking powder).
● 1 egg aerates its own weight of flour.
● 1oz (25 grams) of baking powder aerates 1 lb (450 grams) flour.
● However for sponges the combination is different.
● If you put in two eggs you need 2oz (50 grams) soft flour and 2oz (50 grams) caster sugar.
● This means that eggs weighing 4oz (100 grams) need 4oz (100 grams) of solids to balance.

Milk and Cream

● Milk contains approximately ¾ oz (21 grams) of cream per pint (35 grams per litre).
● Single cream contains 18 per cent cream.
● Whipping cream contains 36 per cent cream.
● Double cream contains 48 per cent cream.
● If you whip double cream without adding ½ the quantity of single cream it will curdle and eventually turn to butter.
● If you have no single cream then add 10 per cent milk. Single cream by itself will not whip. However, if you add ½ oz (15 grams) gelatine to 1 oz (25 grams) sugar dissolved in 2fl oz (50mls) hot milk, you could blend it in to single cream and whip. After cooling this will give a reasonable result.

Thickening

● To thicken a sauce you need a minimum of 4 per cent starch.
● If you use a roux you need 5 per cent plain flour and 5 per cent fat.
● To thicken gravy you should add 24 grams cornflour.

Jellies
- To gel fruit juices you need at least ¾oz (22.5 grams) per pint or 4 per cent.
- To set jam you need 1 per cent pectin in the jam ingredients.

Colouring
- You can improve colour of sauces, jam, jellies or cake by the use of natural or artificial colourings:
  Green...Spinach juice or colouring
  Red...Cochineal colouring, raspberry juice, beetroot juice with vinegar
  Yellow...Turmeric, saffron or egg yolks
  Black...Black treacle or gravy colouring
- It goes without saying that you don't usually put a sweet colour in a savoury dish, e.g. raspberry juice in a salad.

Calories

Calories are given for the raw weight before cooking and allowance has been made for fat absorption. 1oz = 25g.

1oz apples	10	1oz chocolate milk	165
1oz asparagus	5	1oz chocolate plain	155
1oz aubergine	5	1oz cod	20
1oz avocado pear	25	1oz cornflour	100
		1oz courgettes	3
1oz bacon		1oz crab boiled	35
lean fried	120	1oz cream	
lean grilled	105	double	130
streaky fried	140	single	60
streaky grilled	120	1oz cucumber	3
1oz banana peeled	30		
1oz baked beans	25	2oz egg boiled (1 med)	90
broad fresh	10		
runner fresh	4	1oz flour white	100
1oz beef lean raw	50	wholemeal	95
1oz beetroot cooked	15		
1oz blackberries	10	1oz grapefruit	5
1oz blackcurrants	10	1oz grapes	15
1oz bread, white or brown	70		
1oz bread fried	200	1oz haddock	20
1oz butter	225	1oz ham lean boiled	35
		1oz herring	65
1oz cabbage	5	1oz honey	80
1oz carrots	5		
1oz cauliflower	5	1oz lemon with peel	4
1oz celery	3	1oz lentils dried	85
1oz cheese		1oz lettuce	3
blue	105		
camembert	90	1oz mackerel	30
cheddar	120	1oz margarine	225
cottage	30	1oz melon	5
cream	130	1 pint milk	370
curd	40	1oz mincemeat	75
edam	90	1oz mushrooms uncooked	2
gruyère	130	fried	60
parmesan	120		
stilton	100		
1oz chicken uncooked	35		
roast	40		

1 oz nuts	150-170
1 oz oil	260
1 oz olives	25
1 oz onions uncooked	5
fried	100
spring	10
1 oz oranges	10
1 oz oysters, shelled	15
1 oz parsley	5
1 oz pasta	100
1 oz peaches fresh	10
1 oz peanut butter	175
1 oz peanuts	170
1 oz pears fresh	10
1 oz peas fresh	20
1 oz peppers red or green	10
1 oz pineapple fresh	15
tinned in syrup	20
1 oz potatoes	
raw, baked or boiled	25
1 oz instant potato	
powder	105
1 oz prawns	
shelled and boiled	30
1 oz radishes	4
1 oz raisins	70
1 oz raspberries fresh	5
tinned in syrup	30
1 oz rice	100
1 oz salad cream	100
1 oz scallops	30
1 oz strawberries	5
1 oz sugar	110
1 oz sweetcorn	30
1 oz tomatoes	4
fried	20
1 oz walnuts	155
1 oz watercress	4

1 plain yoghurt	
(small carton)	80
1 fruit yoghurt	
(small carton)	140

Coupe California

A refreshing fruit starter to whet the appetite

Ingredients

peaches 4 fresh
plums 4 fresh
cherries 8
lettuce 4 leaves
yoghurt 5fl oz/150ml
lemon juice and grated rind
   of 1
honey 1 tsp

Preparation time 8 mins
Portions 4   **Calories per portion** 164

Method

1 Slice the peaches and plums, and stone the cherries.
2 Place the shredded lettuce in 4 glasses, leaving room for the fruit.
3 Mix the fruit together and pour onto lettuce.
4 Mix the yoghurt, honey and lemon juice together to form a dressing.
5 Serve.

3 Mash the pulp of the avocado and blend with mayonnaise. Add lime juice, salt and pepper, and chopped celery. Add ginger and mix thoroughly.
4 Top the oranges with the avocado dressing.
5 Serve.

Variations

A Replace the avocado in the dressing with pawpaw or 2 medium size ripe pears.
B Replace oranges with 2 or 3 grapefruit.
C Replace the avocado pulp with cooked apple purée into which you have blended mayonnaise and grated lemon.

Chef's Tips

- there are many types of lettuce that you can use for salad. Use the one that you like best, either for flavour or presentation. Remember lettuces, once picked don't remain fresh for very long, so it's best to use on the day of purchase. Webb lettuce are usually economical and remain crisp longer than most other varieties (chilling helps keep the crispness).
- serve as a very cold starter with lemon sorbet.
- this dish will be suitable to "break up" a big meal, cleansing the palate between a strong first or second course, and a blander main course. In some restaurants alcohol will be added (brandy, orange liqueur, vodka or gin).

Stuffed Grapefruit
With savoury or sweet fillings

Ingredients

grapefruit 2 medium
lettuce leaves 8
prawns peeled (8oz/225g)
mushrooms (5oz/150g) white
   thinly sliced
salt and **pepper**
wine vinegar (2fl oz/50ml)
dill chopped 2 Tbs
salad oil (2fl oz/50ml)
mustard ready mixed
   (½tsp/2.5ml)

Preparation time 15 mins
Portions 4   **Calories per portion** 150

Method

1 Halve the grapefruit, carefully remove the fruit and keep to one side. Throw away pith and pips but keep case.
2 Put the lettuce leaves inside the grapefruit case.

3 Mix the prawns and sliced mushrooms together with the grapefruit and season.
4 Blend the oil, vinegar and mustard.
5 Mix the dressing with the prawns, mushrooms and grapefruit, and fill the grapefruit cases.
6 Sprinkle with chopped dill and serve.

Variations

A Try substituting sliced stuffed olives for the mushrooms.
B Replace the prawns by walnuts and plain white fish.
C Instead of French dressing, try a light, sour cream dressing with a little Stilton cheese.
D Oranges can be used instead of grapefruit.

Chef's Tips

- to spice up the dressing try adding 2 Tbs of gin.
- frozen prawns are quite acceptable, but make sure you don't refreeze them again.
- the acidity of a citrus fruit can be increased by adding lemon juice, or if sweetening is required honey is best.
- try sprinkling brown sugar with a pinch of mixed spice over the grapefruit filling, then glaze under the grill quickly.

Waldorf Salad

Apple, celery, walnuts and lettuce with mayonnaise

Ingredients

apples (8oz/225g) peeled
  cored and diced
celery (8oz/225g) chopped or
  sliced
walnuts chopped (4oz/100g)
lettuce leaves 8
mayonnaise (5fl oz/150g)

Preparation time 15 mins   **Chilling time** 30 mins
Portions 4   **Calories per portion** 500

Method

1 Combine all the ingredients, except the lettuce leaves.
2 Place the lettuce leaves on individual bowls and fill with the
  mixture.
3 Chill and serve.

Variations

A Combine together eating and cooking apples for more flavour.

B For a sweeter variation try some pears with the apples.

C Try adding some spring onions or chives, which will sharpen the flavour.

Chef's Tips

- don't peel the apples. This will give more flavour, and a crunchiness to the salad.
- you can thin down the mayonnaise by adding a little yoghurt.
- to reduce calories substitute low-fat salad dressing for the mayonnaise or low-fat yoghurt.
- eat the salad fresh — it will not improve in the fridge.
- try scooping out big red apples and filling with the salad, finely chopped.
- serve with cold meats, poultry, eggs or fish: goes particularly well with grilled dishes.

Apple Salad
With cucumber, onion and cream cheese

Ingredients

apples 4 eating, cored and
    chopped
cucumber ½ medium
    chopped
spring onions 3 chopped
salad cream 1 Tbs
single cream 2 Tbs
lemon juice 3 Tbs
salt and **black pepper**
lettuce leaves 4 large
cottage cheese (1 lb/450g)
watercress to garnish

Preparation time 10 mins
Portions 8   Calories per portion 300

Method

1 Mix cream and salad cream together with the lemon juice,
  and season to taste.
2 Stir in apples, cucumber and onions.

3 Arrange lettuce leaves on a large serving plate.
4 Place a portion of cheese in each leaf and top with apple and cucumber mixture.
5 Garnish with watercress and serve with brown bread and butter.

Variations

A Omit the apples and replace with peeled pears.
B Add 4oz/100g sliced celery to the basic recipe.
C Use yoghurt instead of the mixture of salad cream and cream.

Chef's Tips

- the best apples for this recipe are Cox's Orange Pippins.
- to increase the acidity, either use more lemon juice or orange juice together with 1 Tbs vinegar.
- for colour use a mixture of unpeeled red and green apples.
- this can be served as a last course, an accompaniment to cold meat dishes or as a sandwich filling.

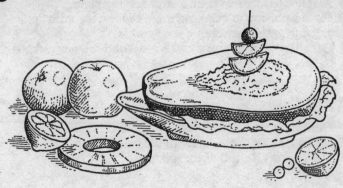

Avocado and Pineapple with Yoghurt

Ingredients

avocado pears 2
pineapple chopped (2oz/50g)
apple chopped (1oz/25g)
fresh ginger chopped
 (½oz/15g)
sugar (½oz/15g) white
salt and pepper
yoghurt (3fl oz/75g)
lemon juice (1fl oz/25ml)
mint chopped 1 tsp
Garnish:
 orange and lemon
  segments
 glacé cherries

Preparation time 15 mins
Portions 4   Calories per portion 170

Method

1 Cut the avocados lengthways and remove stones.
2 Place all other ingredients in a bowl and toss.
3 Leave for 10 minutes, then fill avocados with the mixture.
4 Decorate with slices of lemon and orange on a stick with glacé cherries.

Variations

A Omit pineapple, apple and ginger in filling. Replace with chopped tomato and cucumber.
B Omit pineapple, apple and ginger. Replace with grapefruit segments or oranges or tangerines.
C Use diced melon or peaches and apricots in the filling instead of pineapple and apple.

Chef's Tips

- to make sure an avocado is ripe, cradle one in the palm of your hand. If ripe it should yield to gentle pressure all over. Never use an unripe avocado.
- instead of yoghurt, blend a little apple purée and mayonnaise in equal amounts. Flavour with lemon juice and grated lemon rind.
- with an over-ripe avocado prepare a dip by mashing the pulp and blending it with lemon juice and cream cheese.

Pineapple Cole Slaw
Ingredients

pineapple fresh (8oz/225g)
cabbage white (8oz/225g)
oil 4 Tbs
wine vinegar 2 Tbs
cream 1 Tbs
salt pinch of
ground ginger pinch of
Dijon mustard 1 tsp

Preparation time 15 mins
Portions 4   **Calories per portion** 168

Method

1 Cut pineapple into rings, then chunks, then slice chunks
   into thin strips, and shred the cabbage.
2 Combine the two.
3 Blend dressing and pour onto cabbage and pineapple.
4 Toss and serve.

Variations

A Replace pineapple with apples or pears.
B Use red cabbage instead of white.
C Replace French dressing with a mayonnaise.
D Try using sauerkraut instead of cabbage. In this case omit
vinegar in dressing, and replace with cream.

Chef's Tips

- use fresh pineapple whenever possible. Canned is generally
too sweet.
- add in a chopped, sour apple to the basic mixture to lift the
flavour.
- lemon flavoured mayonnaise goes well with this dish.
- add strips of ham, beef or turkey to give it more substance.

Pineapple Cream Cheese

Pineapple slices with cheese and nut topping

Ingredients

cream cheese or cottage
  cheese (4oz/100g)
peanut butter (2oz/50g)
  smooth
egg yolks 2
salt and **pepper**
chilli pinch of
ginger pinch of ground
pineapple slices4
  preferably fresh
lettuce leaves 4

peanuts (2oz/50g) crushed
  and slightly toasted

Preparation time 10 mins   **Cooking time** 5 mins
  (toasting peanuts)
Portions 4   **Calories per portion** 335

Method

1 Mix in a bowl cream cheese, peanut butter and egg yolks. Add seasoning and spices and mix.
2 Place a lettuce leaf on each pineapple slice and spoon some cheese mixture on top.
3 Sprinkle with chopped peanuts and serve.

Variations

A Replace pineapple by halves of peaches or pears filled with cheese.
B To cream cheese, add chopped chives or a little crushed garlic.
C Blend cream cheese and blue cheese with chopped chives and diced pineapple. Serve on halves of ripe pears.

Chef's Tips

- peanuts can be toasted in a pan under the grill for a few minutes.
- raw pineapple is a good source of vitamin A and C.
- the juice of fresh pineapple has an enzyme that is good for tenderising meat.
- peanut butter can be made easily. Slightly toast peanuts, add the same volume (1 cup peanuts to 1 cup oil/butter) and liquidise to a paste (or mince and pass through a sieve). Keep in airtight jars in the fridge. You can use the same procedure with almonds, walnuts, hazelnuts and so on. The mixture can be sweetened with honey (use unsalted nuts for this) and you can also add melted bitter chocolate for a delicious dessert or a tasty sandwich spread.

9

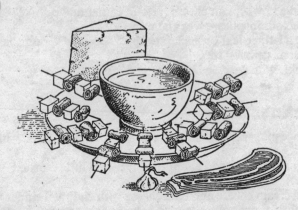

Barbecued Bacon, Cheese and Pineapple Kebab

Ingredients

cheese cheddar or any hard
    cheese (4oz/100g)
bacon (4oz/100g)
pineapple cubes (4oz/100g)
    tinned or fresh
Barbecue sauce:
    soya sauce 3 Tbs
    ginger (½oz/15g) chopped
        fresh
    brown sugar (½oz/15g)
    vinegar 2 Tbs
    oil 3 Tbs
    pineapple juice 2 Tbs

Preparation time 45 mins   **Cooking time** 8
Portions 4   **Calories per portion** 186

Method

1 Cut up all ingredients — cheese, bacon, and pineapple — in cubes.
2 Place two pieces of each on six skewers or sticks.
3 Combine all barbecue sauce ingredients, and liquidise.
4 Soak the kebabs in sauce for 30 minutes.
5 Sauté or quickly grill kebabs to obtain a browning without melting the cheese.
6 Serve hot or cold.

Variations

A Substitute cubed cooked lean ham or gammon with diced cooked turkey or chicken. Or else you can use a combination of ham and turkey, or ox tongue and turkey.
B Substitute for pineapple pieces of apple.
C Instead of barbecue sauce try a rich, lemon-flavoured mayonnaise spiced with a pinch of cayenne pepper.
D These small kebabs can also be rolled in flour and beaten egg crumbs or matzo meal and fried like fritters for 30 seconds.

Chef's Tips

• fresh pineapples have greater acidity and should be used in preference to canned, but canned pineapple cubes and juice (the latter is usually sweetened) can be used.
• if using raw bacon scald it first for 30 seconds in boiling water then skewer as in recipe.
• if using stale or bland cheese spread on it a little English mustard.

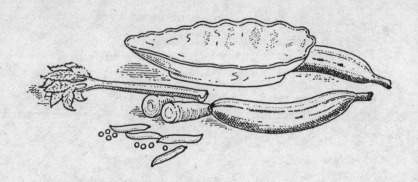

Banana and Chicken Mayonnaise

Ingredients

bananas (3 lbs/1½kg)
chicken (6oz/175g) cooked
  and off the bone
peas (4oz/100g) cooked
carrots (4oz/100g) cooked
celery 1 stick
salt and **pepper** to taste
paprika pinch of
lime juice of half
mayonnaise (4fl oz/100ml)

Preparation time 10 mins
Portions 8   **Calories per portion** 185

Method

1 Cut up the chicken and carrots, and chop the celery.
2 Peel the bananas and slice.

3 Add the lime juice to the bananas.
4 Place the chicken, peas and carrots in a bowl. Add the bananas and celery, and blend in the mayonnaise.
5 Season and serve (on lettuce leaves).

Variations

A Instead of chicken, use the same quantity of prawns, and add some crushed peanuts.
B Flavour with pineapple juice instead of lime.
C Instead of ripe bananas, use green unripe ones. Peel them, boil for 20 minutes, then slice, and proceed as in the basic recipe.

Chef's Tips

- to spice this up, you can add some Stilton cheese to the mayonnaise.
- instead of mayonnaise you can use salad cream (and if you are weight-conscious use slimmer's salad cream).
- if a recipe calls for a certain weight of a *cooked* ingredient, remember that the uncooked weight will be about 25% more.

Baked Apples
Stuffed with cream cheese, nuts and pear

Ingredients

apples 4 large cooking
cream cheese (2oz/50g)
bread crumbs (2oz/50g)
    white
pear 1 conference
walnuts (2oz/50g) chopped

Preparation time 10 mins   **Cooking time** 40 mins
Portions 4   **Calories per portion** 230

Method

1 Core the apples.
2 To the cream cheese, add the nuts, crumbs and the pulp of
   the pear. Mix in well.
3 Score round apples to prevent skin from splitting during
   cooking.
4 Fill core of apples with pear, nut and crumb mixture.
5 Bake at 180 °C/350 °F/Gas Mark 4 for 30-40 minutes until
   cooked.
6 Serve with a wedge of lemon.

Variations

A Cream cheese can be replaced with scrambled egg or a mixture of both.

B Replace cream cheese with a paste made from any kind of cheese — hard or soft. Stilton is good for flavour.

C Peanuts or hazelnuts can replace walnuts.

D The stuffed apple can also be wrapped in short or puff pastry and baked in a similar way until cooked. In this case serve with some cream.

E The reverse can be done with ripe, uncooked pears used for the shells and apples for the stuffing.

Chef's Tips

- it's important that the pear in this recipe should be ripe and easy to mash. Also, the riper the pear the more flavour it will have. Otherwise poach the pear in salted water until tender.
- you can eat this for a dessert or as a snack.
- the acidity of an apple determines its flavour; if using bland-tasting apples add some lemon juice; to add piquancy throw in a pinch of chilli pepper or ginger.

Prawn, Pineapple and Rice Salad

Ingredients

rice ½ cup (4oz/100g)
   long grain
mayonnaise ½ cup
   (4fl oz/100ml)
lemon juice 1 tsp
soya sauce 1 tsp
salt and **pepper**
paprika a pinch
onion 1 small chopped
pineapple rings 3 canned
red cherries ¾ cup (3oz/75g)
prawns (6oz/175g) shelled
cashew nuts (1oz/25g)
mango chutney 3 Tbs

Preparation time 15 mins   **Cooking time** 20 mins
Portions 6   **Calories per portion** 230

Method

1 Boil the rice in salted boiling water until tender (about 20 min).
2 Drain and refresh in cold water. Drain again.
3 Mix together the mayonnaise, lemon juice and soya sauce in a bowl. Stir in the onion and chutney and add the rice.
4 Season with salt and pepper.
5 Cut the pineapple rings into chunks and mix in the mayonnaise. Add the prawns and cherries. Then add the nuts and serve.

Variations

A Omit the cherries and replace them with fresh seedless grapes or olives. Or replace the cashew nuts with walnuts.
B Omit the prawns, and replace with the same quantity of baked beans, peas and corn.
C Substitute a fish of your choice for the prawns.

Chef's Tips

- add a diced hard-boiled egg to the salad.
- Uncle Ben's American rice (or thick plum grain) is very good for this type of salad.
- the colour of the salad can be improved by putting a little turmeric powder into the dressing.

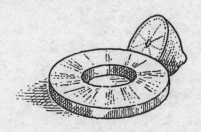

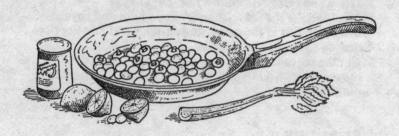

Mushrooms with Yoghurt

Raw mushroom salad with various dressings

Ingredients

button mushrooms
(1 lb/450g)
oil (2fl oz/50ml) vegetable
lemons juice of 2
celery (1oz/25g) chopped
fennel (1oz/25g) chopped
coriander seeds 1 pinch
salt and **pepper**
yoghurt plain (5fl oz/150ml)
parsley a pinch
mint a pinch of fresh

Preparation time 8 mins
Portions 6   **Calories per portion** 105

Method

1 Toss the washed, drained and wiped raw mushrooms in oil
for a few minutes.
2 Add lemon juice and seasoning.

3 Blend in yoghurt, and remaining ingredients.
4 Sprinkle with chopped herbs and serve.

Variations

A Instead of button mushrooms try this recipe with tiny onions instead.

B Add French dressing to the mushrooms instead of celery, fennel and yoghurt.

C Soak the mushrooms in white wine. Then serve with French dressing and lemon juice.

Chef's Tips

- instead of using yoghurt cook (briefly) or marinade the mushrooms in white wine. Then add spices, oil etc.
- mushrooms are perfectly edible raw.
- when adding French dressing to a raw mushroom (or tomato or cucumber) salad wait until 10 mins before you are going to eat it — otherwise the salad will become soggy.

Baby Marrow Salad

With tomatoes, eggs, peppers, onions and olives

Ingredients

baby marrows 8
tomatoes (8oz/225g) sliced
eggs 4 (hard-boiled)
green pepper 1
onions (2oz/50g) chopped
black olives 8
Dressing:
   oil 3 Tbs
   lemon juice 2 Tbs
   yoghurt 3 Tbs
   salt and **pepper** to taste

Preparation time 15 mins   **Cooling time** 5 mins
Portions 8   **Calories per portion** 120

Method

1 Scrape and wash the baby marrows. Cut into slices
  ¼ inch/5mm thick or into chips.
2 Place marrow slices in boiling water for 2 minutes.

3 Then place in a shallow dish and cool.
4 Arrange with sliced pepper, tomato and egg in alternate
rows.
5 Prepare dressing by mixing ingredients.
6 Season and serve.

Variations

A Use a large marrow. Peel, de-seed and boil for 4 minutes.
Coat with an asparagus-flavoured French dressing, which
is made by liquidising 4oz/100g of cooked asparagus with
½ cup of French dressing.
B Serve lightly-boiled courgettes instead of baby marrows,
and use a lemon-flavoured mayonnaise.
C Sauté sliced courgettes in a little oil, together with sliced
aubergines, peppers, onions and tomatoes. Cook for
15 minutes, and serve as a salad after cooling.

Chef's Tips

- make sure you pour the dressing on at the last minute. Do
  not store this salad or dressing as the dish will spoil.
- do not cook for more than 2 mins at most (except
  Variation C). It is better underdone: you can scald for
  only 1 min in boiling salted water. It should still be slightly
  crunchy.
- if young marrows are used they need not be peeled. Older
  ones can be lightly scraped.

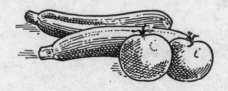

Cucumber Salad

With olives, red peppers and a mint dressing

Ingredients

cucumber (1lb/450g) peeled
   thinly and sliced
mint 2 Tbs chopped fresh
red peppers (4oz/100g)
green and black olives
(5oz/150g)
olive oil 3 Tbs
vinegar 1½ Tbs
salt and **pepper**
French dressing
   (4fl oz/100ml)

Preparation time 10 mins
Portions 6   Calories per portion 142

Method

1 Lie alternate slices of cucumber and slices of red pepper in a shallow dish.
2 Prepare the French dressing, season, and pour over the vegetables.

3 Sprinkle on chopped fresh mint, and decorate with alternate rows of green and black olives.

Variations

A Omit red peppers and used sliced tomatoes instead.
B Replace the French dressing with yoghurt and lemon juice, or a sour cream dressing.
C Transform this into a kind of gazpacho soup. Omitting the olives, liquidise, and add 2 cups of water, and 4oz/100g breadcrumbs. When serving put some extra diced cucumber and red pepper, together with the olives on a side plate.

Chef's Tips

- for the best results use young seedless cucumbers.
- the peel of a cucumber need not be wasted — use it to flavour fruit juices, wine cups or minced (or liquised) and blended with potato soup.
- cucumber can be peeled and then sliced across-ways, cut into half lengthways then into 2in/5cm chunks or into smaller "chips" ¼in/5mm thick.

Cream Cheese and Cucumber Salad

Ingredients

cream cheese (½lb/225g)
red pepper 1 chopped
lemon juice of 1
oil (2fl oz/50ml)
onion (1oz/25g) chopped
cucumber 1 peeled
garlic 1 clove finely chopped
vinegar 1 Tbs
parsley a pinch chopped
mint a pinch fresh
salt and **pepper** to taste

Preparation time 10 mins
Portions 8   **Calories per portion** 230

Method

1 Mash the cheese and add seasoning, lemon juice, crushed garlic, and half the red pepper.
2 Dice the cucumber and mix with the cheese.

3 Toss the mixture in oil together with lemon juice or vinegar.
4 Sprinkle on chopped onion, parsley and mint.
5 Decorate with the rest of the chopped red pepper and serve.

Variations

A Instead of cream cheese, use blue cheese.
B Diced hard cheese can also be used in a similar way, in combination with cucumber, pepper and onions.
C Try adding diced, boiled ox tongue or ham, or some salt beef. In this case flavour with French dressing.

Chef's Tips

- there are many cream cheeses on the market; for this dish it is best to use goat or ewe cheese.
- for a stronger flavour use a combination of Stilton cheese and double cream.
- if you want to use left-over stale cheese: grate the cheese and blend in an equal amount of white sauce.

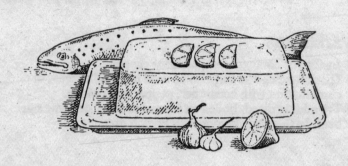

Salmon Pâté

Ingredients

salmon (1 lb/450g) fresh raw or frozen
Marinade:
   dry martini or **cinzano** (¼ pint/150ml)
   lemon juice of ½
   garlic 1 clove crushed
   ginger (½oz/15g) fresh peeled
   onion 1 small (2oz/50g)
   sesame oil 2 Tbs
   soya sauce 1½ Tbs
   honey 2 Tbs
   salt 1 tsp
   pepper a pinch
   cayenne a pinch
   paprika a pinch

Fish paste:
   cod or **haddock** raw (½lb/225g) filleted
   yoghurt (¼ pint/150ml) plain
   onion (2oz/50g) chopped
   bread crumbs (2oz/50g) white
   fennel (3oz/75g) chopped
   leaf spinach (1 lb/450g) blanched drained and dried
   butter (1 oz/25g)
Seasoning:
   salt 1 tsp
   eggs 2
   white pepper a pinch

Preparation time 1 hour (24 hours before serving)   **Cooking time** 1 hour
Portions 20 × 2oz/50g   **Calories per portion** 140

Method

1 Clean and scale salmon. Wash it in cold water. Remove bone and skin. Cut salmon into thin slices.
2 Liquidise marinade and pour over salmon. Leave for 30 mins. Then drain off liquid and keep it for sauce.
3 Skin, wash and drain cod or haddock. Mince the fish to a paste, and blend in yoghurt, eggs, melted butter and seasoning.
4 Mix chopped fennel with spinach. Season to taste.
5 Butter the bottom of two one-pint aluminium or earthenware dishes) each oblong 8" × 3½" wide × 2" deep) or one 2 pint/1000ml container. Place slices of salmon in bottom. Cover with a layer of the white fish paste and scatter the spinach and fennel on top. Repeat the layers until all ingredients are used up. Top the mixture with the white fish paste, and pour over the remaining marinade.
6 Place dish in a shallow tray, half filled with water. Bake for 1 hour at 350 °F/180 °C/Gas Mark 4. Leave to cool.
7 Refrigerate overnight. Make sure pâté is covered with foil.
8 Next day remove pâté from dish and turn out onto a flat dish.
9 Serve.

Variations

A Replace salmon with raw ham (minced and unsalted).
B Replace salmon with a combination of ham and turkey.
C Replace salmon with a mixture of finely-chopped hard-boiled egg and cream cheese.

Chef's Tips

• when baking it is best to put dish in a tray half-filled with water. This ensures that the pâté will not dry out.
• if you add up the ingredients remembering that 1 pint (20fl oz/600ml) of volume equals 20oz in weight (i.e. 1fl oz per 1 oz) you can calculate the size of container that you will need.

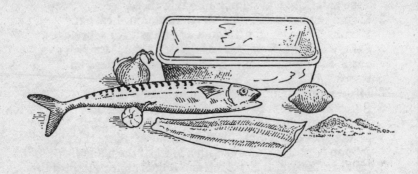

Smoked Mackerel Pâté

Ingredients

smoked mackerel fillets
   (1 lb/450g) — skinned and
   washed
onions (2oz/50g) chopped
horseradish sauce (1oz/25g)
   creamed
egg 1 hardboiled and
   chopped
butter (4oz/100g) melted
garlic 1 clove chopped
paprika a pinch of
cayenne a pinch of
lemon juice and grated rind
   of one
breadcrumbs (2oz/50g)
   white

Preparation time 15 mins
Portions 16 × 2oz   **Calories per portion** 110

Method

1 Mince the mackerel and the onions.
2 Mix all the other ingredients in a bowl, adding the melted butter last.
3 Combine all ingredients together, and fill small ramequin dishes (small, round ovenware soufflé dishes about 3"/7.5cm wide and ½"/1cm deep) with the mixture.
4 Pour a little melted butter on top to seal, and chill.
5 Serve

Variations

A Replace the smoked mackerel with either smoked trout or, if you're feeling extravagant, smoked salmon.
B Instead of butter, add the same amount of mayonnaise.
C Replace the butter with whipped double cream or cream cheese.
D To transform this into a mousse, dissolve 2oz/50g gelatine in one cup of hot white sauce. Reheat all ingredients and mix with the sauce. Simmer for 10 minutes. Then pass through a sieve and cool. For every cup of cold mixture fold in half a cup of whipped cream. Chill in moulds.

Chef's Tips

- try serving the mackerel pâté with brown bread and a cucumber salad.
- make sure you remove the skin from the mackerel.
- the creamed horseradish sauce adds a little piquancy.
- there is no need to sieve or mince the mackerel — mash with a fork. If you want it to be smoother then liquidise.
- mackerel pâté will keep in the fridge for a week, or will freeze.

19

Fish Roe Pâté

A Greek starter

Ingredients

garlic 2 cloves
cod's roe (4oz/100g) smoked
haddock fillet (4oz/100g)
   smoked
breadcrumbs 1 small cup
   (4oz/100g) white
soured cream (4oz/100g)
salad oil 1 small cup
   (4fl oz/100ml)
egg yolk 1

lemons juice and grated rind
   of 2
salt and pepper and paprika
   to taste
Garnish:
   olives 4 or 5 (2oz/50g)
   sliced
pickled gherkins 2 (2oz/50g)
   sliced

Preparation time 6 mins   Cooking time 10 mins
   Waiting time   2 hours
Portions 12   Calories per portion 180

Method

1 Poach haddock fillet in a little water for ten minutes. Cool
   and drain.
2 Put a third of all ingredients in the liquidiser at top speed.
   Or put through a mincer (as fine as possible).

3 Add another third into the liquidiser and so on until mixture is completely liquidised or minced (the result will look like an off-colour mayonnaise).
4 Serve on a shallow dish. Decorate on top with olives cut in slices and small gherkins.

Variations

A If you've just won a lottery add 2oz caviar to the mixture. Serve with small muffins or small yeast pancakes and brown bread. Red herring roes, or any pink fish roes, can be used.
B Alternatively use smoked trout fillets instead of the haddock and cod's roe. Flavour fish with a slurp of whisky, and instead of the breadcrumbs, go north of the border and use porridge oats; to complete, serve on toasted Scotch Bath Bun.
C Replace the roe and haddock by the same amount of smoked salmon and cooked salmon (canned is good enough). Leave out the garlic but add 2 Tbs of Pernod for a special flavour.

Chef's Tips

- if smoked haddock is not available use other smoked fish (like mackerel or kippers).
- if the fish is too salty soak in water for one hour before cooking or cook in milk.
- colour can be further improved by the use of tomato purée.
- make sure you chill the mixture for 2 hours before serving.
- 1oz melted gelatine can be added — it will produce a set and smoother texture.

20

Chicken Liver Pâté

A light, traditional liver pâté.

Ingredients

chicken livers (1 lb/450g)
salt 2 level tsp (10g)
potassium nitrate (saltpeter)
  2g (optional — see
  Chef's tips)
bacon rashers streaky
  (8oz/225g) diced with rind
  removed, desalted
pork sausage meat
  (8oz/225g)
egg 1
flour (2oz/50g)
black pepper a pinch
mace a pinch of ground

paprika a pinch of ground
bay leaves 2
thyme a pinch of ground
brandy (2fl oz/50ml)
chicken fat (2oz/50g) or
  butter or lard
onions (2oz/50g) chopped
Note: use two aluminium-
foil moulds (as used in take-
away restaurants)
7½ inch × 3½ inch
high × 2inch deep (ovenware
will do just as well)

Preparation time 70 mins   Cooking time 1½/2hours
Portions16 × 2oz4   Calories per portion 200

Method

1 Clean livers, (and if necessary remove the sack of gall
  without bursting). Wash in salted water. Drain and mince.
2 Add salt and saltpeter, and leave for 60 mins.
3 Heat chicken fat or butter, and fry chopped onions with
  the bacon for 3 mins. Don't brown too much.

4 Mince all ingredients together, except bay leaves.

5 Place the bay leaves in the bottom of a well-greased shallow casserole — about 1½ lb/720g size. Fill with the mixture.

6 Cover dish with foil and place in a tray half filled with hot water to produce steam. Bake at 350 °F/180 °C/Gas Mark 4 for 1¼ to 1½ hours. The pâté is cooked when a knife or needle inserted into it comes out clean (like a cake test).

7 The pâté must be compressed so it is not loose and crumbly; if the top of the pâté is higher than the sides of the dish, when you take it out of the oven, put a chopping board on top of the dish, and put something heavy on the chopping board, so the pâté cools under pressure. If the top of the pâté is below the side of the dish place a piece of cardboard on the top of the pâté and a heavy weight on the cardboard.

8 When cool melt a little chicken fat or clarified butter and pour on top of the pâté. This will seal it and prevent it from drying out.

Variations

A Instead of chicken livers, use calf or lambs liver without skin or nerves.

B You can substitute sausage meat with the minced raw meat e.g. veal, turkey, lamb, beef, or game.

C Reduce the quantity of onions, and use more garlic. Mushrooms too give a good flavour but tend to brown the pâté.

Chef's Tips

● the use of saltpeter is to make the liver a good pink colour. If you are going to feed the pâté to young children omit it altogether, and in any case, only use a pinch. Too much is bad for you. It is also a preservative.

● if you want the pâté to have a softer texture, then sauté the liver before mincing, and for a smooth pâté, add some whipped cream, together with some stock. For every two cups of pâté, one cup of cream and 2 to 3 Tbs of stock. If you want a creamy pâté remember to remince the cooked pâté before adding the cream and stock.

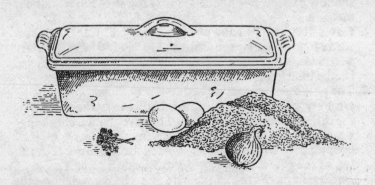

21

Lamb Pâté

Ingredients

lamb (1 lb/450g) minced raw
onions (2oz/50g) chopped
eggs 2 medium
flour (2oz/50g)
butter (2oz/50g)
lambs liver (4oz/100g)
minced
salt and **pepper**
mace a pinch of ground
ginger a pinch of ground
mint 1 Tbs fresh chopped
walnuts (3oz/75g) chopped
pistachio nuts (2oz/50g) or
    skinned broad beans
bay leaves 3

Preparation time 15 mins   **Cooking time** 1½ hours
Portions 16 × 2oz   **Calories per portion** 125

Method

1 Blend all the ingredients together.
2 Place in a shallow, well-greased dish, aluminium or earthenware dishes (2 × 1 pint or 1 × 2 pints), with unmelted butter.
3 Place a lid on top and bake at 350 °F/180 °C/Gas Mark 4 for 1½ hours.
4 Cool and chill.
5 Serve cold with salads.

Variations

A Substitute lamb for chicken, turkey or duck, and the lamb's liver for chicken liver.
B Replace the minced lamb with lean and fat pork in equal quantities, and use pig's liver instead of lamb's liver.
C Replace lamb with veal and instead of lamb's liver, use calf's liver.

Chef's Tips

- margarine can be used instead of butter (or any kind of fat).
- with chicken livers make sure you remove the gall without bursting, as the liquid will make the meat taste very bitter.
- for a well-seasoned paté remember to use salt in the following proportion: ¼oz/8g per pound (450g) of meat used, and pepper ⅛ tsp(1g) per pound (450g) of meat.

22

Avocado and Prawn Mousse

Ingredients

chicken stock ½ cube
water 1 cup (5fl oz/150ml)
gelatin (1oz/25g)
anchovy essence 1 tsp
tomato purée 1 Tbs
   (1oz/25g)
margarine (½oz/15g)
flour 1 tsp (½oz/15g)
avocado pears 3 ripe
double cream 1 large cup
   (6fl oz/180ml) whipped
salt, pepper, paprika, garlic
   salt pinch of each
prawns 1 cup (4oz/100g)
   frozen
butter 1 Tbs (1oz/25g)

sweet martini 1 sherry glass
   (2fl oz/50ml)
lemon juice of half
stuffed olives 4 (1oz/25g)
   black
mint leaves 2 finely chopped
   fresh

Preparation time 30 mins   **Chilling time** 1 hour
Portions 6   **Calories per portion** 350

Method

1 Dissolve the chicken cube, gelatine and anchovy essence in a cupful of boiling water.
2 Add tomato purée to make a basic stock.
3 Make a sauce by cooking margarine and flour until a sandy texture is produced. Gradually add stock while stirring, then cool.
4 Cut each avocado in two, and remove the stone. Scoop out the flesh and blend this pulp with the sauce. Pass through a sieve or liquidiser. To the purée add whipped cream, then season to taste and chill.
5 Toss the prawns in butter for a few minutes to evaporate moisture and develop flavour. Add 1 Tbs sweet Martini. Boil for 1 min then add lemon juice. Cool quickly, then gently mix the cooked prawns into the mousse mixture.
6 Neatly fill each half of avocado with the mixture and decorate with a few stuffed olives, mint leaves or dill.

Variations

A Replace avocado with pawpaw and follow the same procedure.
B Cook and liquidise to a purée one cup of ratatouille (4oz/100g). Blend it into the avocado purée and proceed as before.
C Purée one cup of cooked chicken and blend it into the avocado pulp. Add aspic jelly, (2 tsp diluted in ½ cup boiling water, blend into purée, cool and) fill avocado skins as before. Decorate with pieces of red pepper.

Chef's Tips

• add whipped cream only when avocado has been blended into the jelly and has been chilled.
• avocado pears must be ripe to be edible.
• because avocado pears are high in fat content, a sharp flavour (lemon or lime juice) goes well with them.

23

Pineapple Dip

Cubes of pineapple with six varieties of dips and sauces

Ingredients

pineapple 1 fresh, peeled, cored and cut in cubes.
Preparation time for each dip 12-15 mins.

Dip 1
cream cheese 2oz/50g
salad cream 2 Tbs
mango chutney 2 Tbs
curry powder pinch of
lime or **lemon** juice 1 Tbs
salt and **pepper**
Portions 2   Calories per portion 135

Method
Mix all ingredients into a smooth paste.

Dip 2
avocado pulp (3oz/75g)
blue cheese (1oz/25g)
lemon juice of 1
spring onion 4 small (total weight 1oz/25g) chopped
ginger and **paprika** a pinch chopped
garlic 1 clove chopped
Port wine 1 Tbs
Portions 3   **Calories per portion** 145

Method
Combine all the ingredients together to form a smooth paste.

Dip 3
cream cheese (3oz/75g)
peanuts (2oz/50g) chopped
onions (2oz/50g) chopped
orange juice and grated rind of ½
lime juice and grated rind of ½
cayenne pepper a pinch
Portions 3   **Calories per portion** 250

Method
Combine ingredients to make a soft paste

Dip 4
cream cheese (3oz/75g)
tomato pulp (2oz/50g) fresh from 1 large tomato
avocado pulp (4oz/100g) from 1 avocado
spring onion 1 oz/25g chopped
paprika a pinch
salt
pepper
lemon juice of 1
Portions 4   **Calories per portion** 160

Method
Mix all ingredients together and pass through a sieve

Dip 5
cream cheese (6oz/175g)
onion (1oz/25g) chopped
caraway seeds 1 tsp
salt and **pepper** to taste
celery salt a pinch
Portions 4   **Calories per portion** 200

Method
Combine all ingredients and pass through a sieve.

Dip 6
aubergine 1 (8oz/225g) peeled if preferred
cream cheese (3oz/75g)
oil 1 tbs
salt and **pepper**
flour 1 Tbs
cayenne a pinch
garlic 2 cloves chopped
lemon juice of 1
Portions 3   **Calories per portion** 240   **Cooking time** 2 mins

Method

1 Slice aubergine lengthways and pass in seasoned flour.
2 Heat oil, and pan fry for 1 min.
3 Liquidise cooked aubergine, and blend remaining
   ingredients.
4 Season to taste.

Chef's Tips

- when using fresh garlic use a garlic press; if garlic is dry
  add 1 tsp oil per 2 cloves of garlic to garlic press as you
  squeeze. The oil brings out the flavour of the garlic.
- to keep garlic, peel the cloves, place in airtight jar with oil
  (weight for weight) in fridge.
- garlic can be frozen, either by placing in airtight jars as
  above or make a paste with oil or butter and freeze.

24

Scrambled Egg with Tomato and Cucumber

Delicious variations on a quick and simple dish

Ingredients

eggs 8 medium
cream 1 Tbs
butter (2oz/50g)
salt and **pepper** to taste
tomatoes 4 medium
cucumber 1 small
oil (1 fl oz/25ml)
toast 4 pieces

Preparation time 5 mins   **Cooking time** 5 mins
Portions 4   **Calories per portion** 450

Method

1 Beat eggs with cream and season with salt and pepper.
2 Heat butter in a thick bottomed pan, and cook over a
   gentle heat, stirring continuously until the egg curdles
   uniformly.

3 Peel and deseed cucumber and cut in small cubes.
4 Skin, deseed and chop tomatoes.
5 Mix the tomatoes and cucumber together and sauté for 4 minutes.
6 Make the toast and put 2 spoonfuls of scrambled egg on each piece. Top with tomato mixture.
7 Serve.

Variations

A Instead of the tomato and cucumber, add 2 spoonfuls of crab meat to the scrambled egg, or boiled, shelled prawns.
B Sauté 4oz/100g sliced mushrooms and blend into the scrambled egg.
C Place 4 hot asparagus tips per portion on top of the scrambled egg.

Chef's Tips

- the use of a thick bottomed pan in cooking the scrambled egg is to diffuse the heat evenly and the scrambled egg if stirred gently won't become lumpy or cook unevenly.
- if you have any scrambled egg left over, blend with mayonnaise and some chopped onions, and use as a filling for sandwiches.
- an easy way to make scrambled eggs is to add 1 Tbs cream (single, or double if you want it to be richer) or milk for every 2 eggs beaten up; place eggs and milk/cream in a pan which is put in a tray of boiling water (a bain-marie); whisk from time to time as it begins to set. Any surplus water in the pan can be poured out (it separates from the eggs).

25

Eggs stuffed with Mushrooms

A quick, hot starter (or snack) with endless variations

Ingredients

eggs 8 medium
Filling:
   mushrooms (½lb/225g)
     any variety
   butter (2oz/50g)
   flour (1oz/25g)
   cream (¼ pt/150ml)
   salt a pinch
   pepper a pinch
   ground nutmeg a pinch
   cheese grated (2oz/50g)
     cheddar

Preparation time 15 mins   **Cooking time** 18 mins
Portions 8   **Calories per portion** 190

Method

1 Place eggs in cold water. Bring to the boil and cook for 12 mins. In the meantime prepare the mushrooms.
2 Shell the eggs and cut in halves. Remove the yolks and sieve them.
3 Wash, clean and chop mushrooms. Heat the butter in a pan, and cook mushrooms for 5 mins. Stir in flour and pour in the cream to make a thick sauce.
4 Season, add the egg yolks, and then half the grated cheese. Mix well together.
5 Fill the cavities of the egg halves with this mixture. Sprinkle the rest of the cheese on top, and brown under the grill.

Variations

A Replace the mushrooms with 2oz/50g of canned or fresh salmon. Blend with the egg yolks, cream and mayonnaise to a stiff consistency.
B Replace the mushrooms with cream cheese (2oz/50g).
C Replace the mushrooms with a purée of baked beans in tomato sauce.
D The filling can be made up from many different leftovers.

Chef's Tips

- serve hot or cold with lettuce leaves, or on toast, with a tomato salad and French dressing.
- try with a hot cheese or curry sauce, on a bed of spinach or rice.
- when eggs have boiled you can remove shells and place eggs in cold water to which has been added 10% of its volume of wine vinegar; the eggs can then be kept in the fridge for up to 24 hours until ready to use.
- once you have stuffed the eggs eat them—they do not last well.

26

Cheese soufflé

Individual hot cheese soufflés

Ingredients

butter (1oz/25g)
flour (¾oz/20g)
milk (¼ pint/150ml)
cheddar cheese (1oz/25g)
  grated
parmesan cheese (1oz/25g)
egg yolks 3
egg whites 4
salt and **pepper**
paprika and **cayenne** pepper
  a pinch
cheddar cheese (1oz/25g)
  grated for flavouring
  mixture

Preparation time 10 mins   **Cooking time** 15 mins
Portions 6   **Calories per portion** 175

Method

1 First make a white sauce: melt butter, add flour, and cook to a sandy texture. Gradually stir in cold milk and heat until you have the right consistency.
2 Cool a little, then blend in the rest of the egg yolks, grated cheese and seasoning.
3 Whip the egg whites with a pinch of salt until they peak.
4 Add a little of the sauce into the whipped egg white and beat well.
5 Gently fold in the rest of the mixture.
6 Sprinkle grated cheese inside individual greased moulds and fill to the brim with soufflé mixture. Level with a fork. Sprinkle grated cheese on top as well.
7 Place moulds on a baking tray and bake at 200 °C/400 °F/Gas Mark 6 for 15-20 mins.
8 When they've risen between 1½ and 2½ inches above the mould, and are light brown on top, they should be ready. Serve immediately.

Variations

A Add 2oz/50g of cooked, well-drained and dried leaf spinach, together with 1 clove of garlic and 4 canned anchovy fillets, mashed or chopped to a purée.
B Add 2oz/50g purée of minced ham to basic ingredients. Or chicken if you prefer.
C Add 2oz/50g of chopped cooked white mushrooms and proceed as before.

Chef's Tips

- make sure the egg whites are **folded** into the sauce, not beaten in.
- to ensure an even rising, go round each mould with your finger, leaving a ring about ¼ inch deep all round.
- if you prefer use a bigger mould and make it all in one. But cook for 25-30 mins.

27

Curd-cheese Fritters

Ingredients

milk (4 pints/2.4 litres)
salt 1 tsp
white vinegar (1 fl oz/25ml)
egg 1
white breadcrumbs
(4oz/100g)
salt and **pepper** to taste
curry powder a pinch
oil for deep frying

Preparation time 20 mins   **Drying time** 1 hour
   Cooking time 5 mins   **Chilling time** 30 mins
Portions 6   **Calories per portion** 350

Method

1 Bring the milk to blood heat — do not boil. Cool slightly,
  then mix in the salt and vinegar. Let it settle for a while
  until it forms a curd.

2 Strain curd through a muslin cloth, and squeeze out any surplus moisture.
3 Dry for 1 hour.
4 Squeeze again, and then chill until it becomes firm.
5 Now combine all the ingredients, including the curd, to form a thick paste. Shape into balls.
6 Roll in flour, and deep fry until golden brown.
7 Serve on skewers or cocktail sticks.

Variations

A To the basic curd cheese add chopped onions (1oz/25g) or a clove of chopped garlic.
B Add to the basic mixture chopped walnuts or peanuts (1oz/25g).
C Add chopped mushrooms (1oz/25g).

Chef's Tips

- only half cook the mushrooms. They taste much better and hold their shape better.
- you can liven up these fritters by serving them with olives, cubed pineapple, small pickled onions, or wedges of apples and pears.
- curd cheese can be varied by adding garlic or chopped fresh chervil or chives to taste.
- curd cheese can be used as part of a cheesecake or flan: add 2 beaten eggs per 1 lb (450g) of curd cheese (sweetened to taste) for the top or filling of a cheesecake or flan.

28

Chilled Orange and Mint Soup

Ingredients

orange juice (1 pt/600ml)
pineapple juice
 (¼ pt/150ml)
clove 1
cornflour 1 tsp
sugar 1 tsp
lemons juice of 2
mint 1 sprig

Preparation time 8 mins **Cooking time** 5 mins
Portions 4 **Calories per portion** 90

Method

1 Combine the orange and pineapple juice, and bring to the
  boil.
2 Mix cornflour and sugar together, add a little cold water in
  a bowl, and pour onto the hot juice. Cook for 5 minutes to
  thicken, stirring occasionally.
3 Cool and add lemon juice.
4 Serve in a bowl with a sprig of fresh mint.

Variations

A Use orange juice and substitute brewed tea for the pineapple juice.

B Use apple and orange juice together. Proceed as in basic recipe.

C Use a combination of grape and orange juice.

D Try blackcurrant juice with lemon juice, but check and if necessary adjust for sweetness.

E You can enrich the basic soup (made with any combination of juices) and thicken it in another way. Use 2 egg yolks and 4 Tbs cream per pint of juice. Add 1 Tbs cornflour. Combine in a bowl, add a quarter of the juice, then pour back into the rest of the juice. Bring to the boil until the consistency of a thin custard.

F Thickening can also be done by using instant mashed potato powder (1oz/25g per pint of juice). Combine starch with ½ cup (4fl oz/100ml) of cold single cream. Heat juice to boiling, pour the mash/cream. Cook for 4 mins until soup is clear and smooth. This method takes a little less time than the above one.

Chef's Tips

● you can use over-ripe or surplus fresh fruit liquidised for these dishes.

● soup, with a little cornflour in it, can be kept frozen.

● potato in soup tends to bring out the flavour as well as thicken.

● thickening of soups (and sauces) can be achieved by adding arrowroot or cornflour or instant mashed potato powder or a roux mixture; the roux is made of equal amounts of butter (or fat) and flour cooked together for 1 min without colouring and then added to the soup or sauce in a ratio of 3oz/75g roux to 1 pint/600ml of soup.

29

Cold Cucumber Soup with Yoghurt

Ingredients

cucumber 1 large (1 lb/450g)
yoghurt (1 pint/600ml)
salt and **pepper**
garlic 1 clove crushed or
chives chopped 1 pinch
mint chopped 1 pinch

Preparation time 8 mins
Portions 8   **Calories per portion** 75

Method

1 Peel, seed, and thinly slice cucumber.
2 Sprinkle the sliced cucumber with a large pinch of salt, and drain in a colander.
3 Crush garlic and add to yoghurt. Blend in the cucumber and season (a pinch of chilli pepper can be added if you like).

4 Liquidise and serve.
5 Sprinkle with chopped chives and fresh mint.

Variations

A Replace the cucumber with 4 large over-ripe tomatoes.
These need to be skinned and seeded, and then proceed as
in the basic recipe.
B Combine an equal quantity of peppers (red and green) and
tomatoes. Liquidise and add to the basic soup.
C Replace the cucumbers by aubergines, sliced and sautéed
with onions for 5 minutes. Liquidise and flavour as in
basic recipe.
D Young marrow (zucchini) can be used raw instead of
cucumber, or pickled cucumber or gherkins — but then
use fresh cream to mellow the acidity of the pickles.
E Liquidise whichever variation of ingredients you choose,
chill and serve as a thick soup with snippets of French
bread.

Chef's Tips

- there is no need to peel a green cucumber — the peel
  imparts a fragrant flavour.
- sour cream or fresh cream with a little lemon juice can be
  used instead of yoghurt.
- instead of fresh mint other fresh herbs can be used, (dill,
  lemon balm, chervil).
- spring onions can replace garlic.

30

Cold Cantaloup Melon Soup
Unusual, tropical fruity soup

Ingredients

yellow cantaloup melon
   (10oz/275g)
sugar (1oz/25g)
cinammon 1 pinch
orange juice (4fl oz/100ml)
lemon juice (1fl oz/25 ml)
yoghurt (½ pt/300ml)

Preparation time 10 mins   **Chilling time** 1 hour
Portions 4   **Calories per portion** 100

Method

1 Put spices into the juices and mix together.
2 Dice the pulp of the melon and soak in the juices.
3 Add the yoghurt and mix well.
4 Serve chilled.

Variations

A The melon pulp can be liquidised with the juice, and blended with sour cream instead of yoghurt.

B The pulp of pawpaw can be used instead of melon, substitute lime juice for orange and lemon juice.

C Replace melon with ripe avocado pulp and juice of 1 lemon.

D A French-style melon soup would omit the yoghurt and use cream instead, together with a ½ cup of port.

E Instead of cantaloup you can use Ogen melon (they are sweeter).

Chef's Tips

- make sure when cutting up melon that none of the juice escapes.
- use ripe melons — these have more flavour, although a little honey can be used to improve flavour and sweetness.
- a little fresh ginger added to the basic recipe will hot up the flavour. Add a little mint as well.

31

Tomato and Cucumber juice

A refreshing summer-time starter served in a glass

Ingredients

pure tomato juice
(½ pint 300ml) tinned or
bottled
cucumber (2oz/50g)
sliced unpeeled
lemon juice 1 Tbs
Worcestershire sauce 1 Tbs
salt a pinch

Preparation time 5 mins   **Chilling time** 1 hour
Portions 4   **Calories per portion** 15

Method

1 Liquidise all ingredients together.
2 Chill for one hour.
3 Serve in glasses.

Variations

A Substitute half the amount of tomato juice with the same amount of orange juice.

B Reinforce basic recipe with 3fl oz/75ml vodka.

C Instead of using cucumber, put in a sprig of fresh parsley or mint leaves, or some sliced green pepper (2oz/50g) liquidised with the juice.

D Liquidise together 1 cup diced cucumber, 1 cup tomato juice, 1 cup red and green peppers. Season, add 1 tsp cider vinegar and 2 Tbs cream. Chill and serve. This is more like a cold Spanish soup than a juice.

Chef's Tips

- pure tomato juice in tins or bottles can be found in any supermarket.
- in summer tomatoes can be found soft enough to liquidise and strain to produce a good juice.
- to improve tomato flavour, add a little honey or sugar (1 tsp per pint).
- juice made from fresh tomatoes can be concentrated by cooking for 5 mins.

32

Creamy Chicken Soup

With lemon, mushroom or celery variations

Ingredients

chicken 1 trussed fowl
 (4 lb/1800g)
water (4 pints/2,400ml)
leeks 2 (8oz/225g)
carrot 1 (4oz/100g)
celery 2 sticks (2oz/50g)
bay leaf 1
clove 1

Thickening:
 chicken fat (2oz/50g)
 flour (2oz/50g)
 single cream
  (5fl oz/150ml)
 salt and pepper
 nutmeg 1 pinch of ground

Preparation time 30 mins   **Cooking time** 1 hour 45 mins
Portions 8   **Calories per portion** 65 (if clear soup), 220 (if chicken meat added)

Method

1 Remove surplus fat from chicken before cooking.
2 Place in large pot or saucepan, and cover with cold water.
3 Bring to the boil and remove scum as it rises to the surface.
4 When liquid is clear, add cleaned leeks, carrots cut in two, and celery together with bay leaf and clove.

5 Simmer gently for 1½ hours. When cooked remove chicken and vegetable and serve them as main dish.

6 Chill the stock, and when fat floats on top remove it.

7 Melt 4oz/100g chicken fat in a saucepan, add 4oz/100g flour. Gradually add 3 pints/1800ml of stock, whisking to avoid lumps.

8 Add cream and seasoning. Serve soup. Any stock left over can be used again.

9 The chicken can be served as a main course, or some of the meat can be used as a garnish.

Variations

A This soup can be made into a lemon soup. Omit the cream, but add juice and grated rind of 2 lemons. Blend 2 egg yolks with 1 cup of cold stock, and 1 level Tablespoon of cornflour per 2 pt of stock. Then gradually add this egg mixture to soup away from heat. When well mixed return to heat until it begins to boil, and thicken like a custard.

B For a mushroom soup add 5oz/150g chopped mushrooms to basic soup, and liquidise again. A cream of asparagus soup can be made in the same way with the addition of 5oz/150g asparagus tips.

C Increase celery in basic recipe by ½ lb/225g to produce a chicken and celery soup.

Chef's Tips

• before boiling chicken try roasting it for 20 minutes until slightly browned. This will improve the chicken flavour of the soup.

• this basic recipe can also be used to make a chicken sauce by the addition of more cream.

• if you add chopped/minced vegetables or chicken you can thicken the soup and make it more of a meal.

• in order to freeze the soup you should have cornflour in it—use cornflour instead of plain flour and the texture of the soup will be retained on thawing.

33

Clear Vegetable Soup
With ways of making it thick or meaty

Ingredients

water (3½ pints/2,100ml)
bouquet garni 1
fennel 2 sticks (4oz/100g)
carrots 4 medium
   (12oz/350g)
celery 2 sticks (4oz/100g)
turnips 2 small (½ lb/225g)
onion 1 studded with four
   cloves
leeks 2 (½ lb/225g)
salt and **pepper** to taste

Preparation time 10 mins   **Cooking time** 40 mins
Portions 8   **Calories per portion** 25

Method

1 Clean, peel and cut vegetables in slices or sticks.
2 Put vegetables in water and bring to boil. Add onion and
   bouquet garni.

3 Simmer for 35 minutes (until vegetables are cooked).
4 Remove bouquet garni.
5 Serve soup with slices of french bread and vegetables as garnish.

Variations

A To turn this into a beef consommé do the following. Take some beef bones that have been browned in the oven, and 1½ lbs 675g of lean, mildly salted beef. Simmer in 3½ pints water for about two hours, making sure you remove the scum as it appears on the surface. Then add the vegetables, with the exception of the onion with its cloves. Split this in two, and brown in a pan before adding to the stock. When vegetables are cooked, remove meat and veg, strain and serve.

B To the basic clear soup add 7oz/200g shredded white or green cabbage, 7oz/200g cut French beans, and 3oz/75g vermicelli. Make sure these are all cooked separately.

C To turn this clear vegetable soup into a broth, liquidise the vegetables after they have been cooked and removed from the soup, and add back to the soup.

D For a meaty borsch, add 2 small beets (½ lb/225g) to veg in Variation A. Return veg to soup after straining, add some pickled beetroot strips and juice. Check the seasoning, and add a little sugar to counteract any acidity.

Chef's Tips

- always start with cold water, and bring the liquid slowly to boiling point. This prevents the liquid becoming cloudy.
- for a richer flavour shallow-fry the meat first. Then add water. Simmer for 2 hours, add vegetables and cook for another ½ hour.

French Onion Soup

A basic recipe for this traditional popular French soup

Ingredients

oil (2oz/50ml)
onions sliced (1 lb/450g)
water (1½ pts/900ml)
madeira wine
    (¼ pint/150ml)
salt and **pepper** to taste
chicken stock cube 1
Garnish:
    French bread 12 thin slices
        (½ lb/225g)
    egg 1 beaten

Preparation time 10 mins   **Cooking time** 25 mins
Portions 6   **Calories per portion** 285

Method

1 Heat the oil in a saucepan.
2 Slowly shallow-fry onions under a low heat until pale
   brown.

3 Add water and wine.
4 Crumble in stock cube.
5 Boil soup for 15 minutes.
6 Season.
7 Toast the bread, and then spread each slice with grated cheese and egg.
8 Under the grill brown the slices of bread coated with cheese until cheese has melted and is crisp.
9 Add two or three slices of toasted bread to each bowl of soup immediately before serving.

Variations

A Add a beef or chicken stock cube to the water and the onions. This will enhance the flavour.
B Substitute madeira with sherry or white port.
C To make a thick onion soup liquidise stock and onion, and if you wish to make a white onion soup, boil the onions, don't fry them, and add cream or a little mashed potato.

Chef's Tips

- the best cheese to use is Gruyère, Emmental or Parmesan, but good old cheddar will do just as well.
- classic French onion soup always contains sliced onion — never chopped!
- shallow fry the onions in a mixture of butter and oil for a better flavour.
- cheese spread on the slices of bread will toast quickly if you are in a hurry.

35

Leek and Potato Soup
With hot and cold variations

Ingredients

margarine or **butter**
  ¼ of ½ lb pack (2oz/50g)
oil 3 Tbs (1½ fl oz/45ml)
leeks 4 (1 lb/450g)
potatoes 4 large (1 lb/450g)
water (1½ pts/900ml)
milk (1 pint/600ml)
chicken stock cube 1
salt and **pepper** to taste
chicken stock cube 1
chopped chives 1 tsp

Preparation time 15 mins   **Cooking time** 40 mins
Portions 8   **Calories per portion** 225

Method

1 Clean and trim the leeks, and remove wilted leaves; slice the leeks into 1½ inch/4cm lengths, then lengthways to remove any soil when you wash and drain. Then slice in thin strips.
2 Peel potatoes, wash and cut in thick chips, then slice chips into slivers; wash and drain.

3 Heat oil and margarine or butter in a saucepan, and cook vegetables for 5 mins without browning: add water and bring to the boil; crumble chicken cube, and simmer for 30 mins until potatoes are soft.
4 Liquidise mixture or pass through a sieve.
5 Reheat soup to boiling point and add milk; when hot season and serve with a sprinkling of chopped chives or parsley.

Variations

A On serving cut up a roasted leg of chicken (hot), and add strips of meat to the soup. Diced or minced ham can be used instead. In these cases serve with snippets of fried bread.
B When the soup is made, cool, add a cup of whipped cream and chill. Whisk the whole mixture and serve in cups with a sprinkling of chopped chives or the green part of a spring onion. This is a traditional Vichyssoise.
C Add 2 cloves of garlic and 2 Tbs tomato purée to basic recipe.
D To make Soubise soup omit leeks and replace with 5oz/150g spring onions. Halve the quantity of potatoes, and replace with 5oz/150g of cooked noodles. Replace milk with yoghurt. After mixing cooked potatoes, noodles and onions together, beat 2 eggs in a bowl, then add yoghurt, and gradually pour in half the soup. Beat well, add to rest of broth, and reheat before serving.

Chef's Tips

- when you sauté vegetables it is better to keep the lid on the saucepan, before liquid is added.
- for a good flavour use a mixture of clarified butter and pork lard for cooking.

36

Fresh Pea Soup

A basic rich, warming vegetable soup

Ingredients

peas with pods (1 lb/450g)
   fresh
onion (2oz/50g) 1 small
margarine (2oz/50g)
spinach fresh leaves
   (4oz/100g)
water (2 pts/600ml)
salt and **pepper** to taste
sugar 1 tsp
mint chopped 1 tsp
monosodium glutamate
   a pinch

Preparation time 10 mins   **Cooking time** 25 mins
Portions 6   **Calories per portion** 100

Method

1 Wash spinach thoroughly to remove sand.
2 Chop raw peas and pods finely. If you have the equipment, mince them.

3 Heat margarine in a saucepan, and sauté onion without browning for 4 mins.
4 Add spinach and peas, and simmer for 5 mins before adding water.
5 Boil for 15 mins. and season.
6 Liquidise to a purée, and then reheat.
7 Sprinkle on chopped fresh mint.

Variations

A Instead of fresh spinach which makes the soup look very green, use any green-leafed vegetable (lettuce, green cabbage or sorrel leaves).

B For a chick pea soup, replace fresh peas with dried chick peas. You will need more water (2½ pints/1500ml). Soak the peas for 6 hours, and cook in the same water. Remove scum as it rises, and when the broth is clear add a clove of garlic, 1oz/25g of red peppers, a pinch of cumin seed, and the juice and rind of a lemon. Add salt and pepper to taste.

C Follow method in Variation B for a Peas Pudding Soup. Reduce the peas to 7oz/200g and reduce the water to 1 pint/600ml. When broth is clear add a green knuckle of bacon, pickled not smoked (11oz/300g); 1 carrot (3oz/75g); 1 small onion studded with 2 cloves; the green part of 1 leek and a bouquet garni. Boil gently for 1 hour. Remove bacon and bouquet garni, then liquidise remainder, remembering to remove cloves from onion. To the resulting purée add some consommé (10fl oz/300ml), season and reboil. Serve with fried croûtons.

Chef's Tips

- when peas are cooked with their pods, you get more flavour.
- pea soup can be garnished with rice, tapioca or vermicelli, or served with fried croûtons.
- frozen or canned processed peas are an adequate substitute: the flavour can be improved by using bacon stock.

Broad Bean Soup

Thick, hot wintery bean soup and variations

Ingredients

onions (2oz/50g)
broad beans (10oz/275g) —
   use dried or frozen out of
   season
oil (3fl oz/90ml)
peppers chopped (1oz/25g)
garlic 1 clove
cumin powder pinch of
salt and **pepper** to taste
mint chopped 1 Tbs

Preparation time 15 mins   **Cooking time** 40 mins
Portions 6   **Calories per portion** 160

Method

1 Wash the beans if fresh, and if dried, soak overnight.
2 Heat oil and shallow fry onions for 5 mins without
   browning.
3 Add broad beans, stir and cook for 2 mins.

4 Add water, garlic and boil until beans are tender (approx. 30 mins if fresh, or — after soaking — 90 mins if dried).

5 When cooked sieve or liquidise; reheat the purée and liquid and season and serve with chopped fresh mint.

Variations

A Substitute any other kind of bean in the same quantity; e.g. haricot or kidney, white, red or black.

B Instead of broad beans, take a can of baked beans (8oz/225g). Sauté 1 medium size chopped onion and a diced rasher of bacon. Liquidise beans, onion and bacon with 2 pints/1200ml of cold water. Pass the mixture through a sieve. Heat gently and season to taste. Serve.

C For a hot bean soup Mexico style, replace onions in Variation B with 2 sliced red chillies ($\frac{1}{8}$oz/3g each) and 2 sliced green chillies. Omit bacon. Combine all ingredients in a saucepan with water (2 pints/1200ml). Boil for 10 minutes, and then liquidise. Reheat and season with a pinch oregano and chopped parsley. Pour soup into individual bowls. Sprinkle some grated cheese on top and brown under grill. Serve with toast.

Chef's Tips

- the spiciness of these soups can be increased with a good pinch of cayenne pepper or fresh chillies, tabasco sauce or curry powder.
- the fresher the beans you use the more time you will save and the tastier the soup.
- blend a little cream or yoghurt into the finished soup and use marjoram, basil or chervil.
- frozen broad beans can be used too: boil for 10 mins, mince to a purée and add stock or milk to get the right consistency (3oz/75g purée for 1 pint of liquid).

38

Chinese Soup

An easy Chinese cabbage, pineapple and pork soup

Ingredients

oil 3 Tbs (1½ fl oz/45ml)
   vegetable
onions (1oz/25g)
cabbage or cos lettuce or
   Chinese cabbage (2oz/50g)
pineapple (3oz/75g) fresh or
   tinned
roast pork (3oz/75g)
soya sauce 1 Tbs
garlic 1 clove crushed
ginger (½oz/15g) fresh
Stock:
   water (2 pints/1,200ml)
   chicken stock cubes 2
   salt and **pepper**

Preparation time 10 mins   **Cooking time** 35 mins
Portions 6   **Calories per portion** 140.

Method

1 Cut pineapple and pork into very thin strips, and the vegetables into shreds.
2 Heat oil and shallow fry (without browning) the onions, cabbage, pork and pineapple for about 7 mins. Add water, and crumble the stock cubes. Bring to the boil. Simmer for 20 mins and season. Add soya sauce, chopped ginger and garlic last; simmer for 5 more mins.
3 Serve in individual bowls.

Variations

A Use chicken or any white meat as a substitute for pork.
B Instead of cabbage, use shredded spinach, beans or celery (any green vegetable will do).
C To all soups sliced field (grilling or cultivated) mushrooms can be added.

Chef's Tips

- beef and chicken stock cubes can be used as a substitute for soya sauce.
- the soup will have more flavour if you fry the meat before adding the onions (it concentrates the flavour).
- if you haven't got much time these soups are ideal, because all the ingredients are cut into small pieces, thus reducing the cooking time.
- an ideal garnish is Chinese vermicelli or other pasta of your choice.
- remember: all the ingredients must be matchstick sized and stir-fried for the best flavour. For 1 cup of solids then add 2 cups of liquid.

39

Humous and Pitta Bread

A cold purée of chick pea, lemon juice, oil, garlic and sesame
seeds served with pitta bread.

Ingredients for Humous

chick peas 1 can (8oz/225g)
    or dried peas (5oz/150g)
    soaked in 1 pint of water
onion ½ a small (1oz/25g)
lemon juice
    1 cup (6fl oz/175ml)
oil 1 cup (6fl oz/175ml)
garlic 1 Tbs (1oz/25g) —
    chopped

sesame seeds toasted
    1 Tbs (1oz/25g)
salt and black pepper
paprika, chilli powder
    (optional), **turmeric** (to
    improve colour) a pinch of
    each
Worcestershire sauce 1 tsp

Preparation time 5 hours for soaking, then 15 mins
    Chilling time 2 hours   **Cooking time** 5 mins.
Portions 4   **Calories per portion** 500

Ingredients for Pitta

flour (½ lb/225g) bread
salt ½ a level tsp
baking powder 2 level tsp

margarine (1oz/25g)
cold water 1 cup (5fl oz/150ml)
oil for greasing tray

Preparation time 10 mins   **Baking time** 20 mins
Portions 4   **Calories per portion** 150

Note

Pitta is usually unleavened bread. The baking powder can be reduced or omitted, but for western tastes we recommend this version. If you don't like pitta serve with toast or bread rolls.

Method for Humous

1 Start the preparation of the humous first, so it will be chilled when the pittas are ready.
2 Soak chick peas in water overnight; wash away the water and replace.
3 Simmer peas and onion until tender (40 mins); then drain and mince or liquidise to a purée.
4 Place purée in a liquidiser with oil and lemon juice, garlic seasoning, Worcestershire sauce etc, and blend until very fine.
5 Pour into a mould, sprinkle on seasame seeds, and chill for two hours. Serve with hot pitta bread.

Method for Pitta

1 Sift flour with salt and baking powder; rub in the margarine until you have a fine, crumbly mixture; add the cold water to produce a smooth dough. Rest for 30 mins.
2 Divide the dough into balls of about 2oz/50g each about the size of an egg. Flatten each ball with a rolling pin to an oval shaped cake about six inches in diameter and ¼ inch thick.
3 Grease a baking tray and bake at 400 °F/200 °C/Gas Mark 6 for 15 to 20 mins. After the first 10 mins turn the pittas so they cook evenly. Serve hot with the humous.

Variations

A Try with cooked garden peas or canned processed peas instead of chick peas, and flavour with two mint leaves in addition to the other flavourings.
B Add 2oz of lean minced ham to a purée of baked beans. Proceed with same ingredients but use garden peas instead of chick peas. Also blend in a small teaspoonful of English mustard.

40

Sweet and Sour Cucumbers

Ingredients

cucumbers — 1 dozen
5 inches/12 cm long
(1½ lbs/675g)
salt (1oz/25g)
onion 1 large (4oz/100g)
sugar (1 lb/450g)
pepper a pinch
mace a pinch
double cream
(½ pint/300ml)
wine vinegar (½ pint/300ml)
pickling spices (1oz/25g)
dill 1 Tbs

Preparation time 30 mins   **6 hours for sweating**   **Chilling time** 2 hours
Portions 12   **Calories per portion** 230

Method

1 Wash the cucumbers, prick all over with a fork, and slice thinly (¼ inch/5mm).
2 Sprinkle with salt, and cover with a heavy board to extract the cucumbers' juices.
3 Leave for 6 hours, then drain off the liquid into a bowl.
4 Mix in the sugar until it is dissolved.
5 Season with spices, and add vinegar and cucumber slices.
6 Beat the cream until light and blend into mixture.
7 Chill in refrigerator until cold and crisp.
8 Serve.

Variations

A Simply peel the cucumbers, and sprinkle with salt. Leave them to sweat for 30 minutes — then wash off salt, and season in lemon juice and yoghurt.
B Blend peeled, sliced cucumber in soured cream, and add chopped mint and garlic to taste. Serve.
C Thinly slice a peeled cucumber, and blend with a French dressing.

Chef's Tips

- do not season the cucumber in the dressing for too long, as it tends to become soggy.
- an alternative way to cut the cucumber is to cut them in chips. This way you can also pass them in flour and fry for 30 seconds for a hot snack.

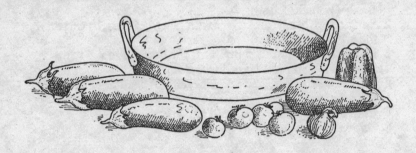

41

Aubergines Turkish Style

Ingredients

aubergines 4 large
   (8oz/225g each)
flour (3oz/75g) plain
   seasoned with ½ tsp each
salt and **paprika**
oil for frying (vegetable)
salt (1oz/25g)
Filling:
   tomatoes (1 lb/450g)
    8 medium
   onion (4oz/100g) 1 large
    chopped

garlic 3 cloves chopped
oil (2fl oz/50ml) vegetable
salt and **pepper**
green pepper 1 medium
   (3oz/75g)
stuffed olives 10 black
parsley 1 tsp chopped
coriander leaves 1 tsp
mint 1 tsp

Preparation time 40 mins   **Cooking time** 10 mins
Portions 4   **Calories per portion** 375

Method

1 Cut the aubergines into four or five slices lengthways.
Sprinkle salt on them and leave for 30 mins. Then wash,
drain well, and pat dry with absorbent paper. Pass in
seasoned flour.

2 Heat oil in a pan, and deep fry the aubergine slices for 1 min. Drain and dry on absorbent paper. Plaçe the aubergines in a flat oval dish.

3 For the filling, heat a little oil in a pan, sauté the chopped onions until soft, but do not brown, and add garlic.

4 Peel, chop and seed tomatoes, and add them to the onion mixture. Cook for 2 mins. Season.

5 Split the green pepper, remove seeds, and cut in thin slices. Simmer for 4 mins in boiling water then blend into the mixture.

6 Cover each slice of aubergine with the mixture. Decorate with stuffed olives and sprinkle on fresh chopped herbs. Serve hot or cold.

Variations

A Cut the aubergines in half. Sprinkle on salt and leave for 20 mins. Wash, drain and dry. Deep fry for 2 mins, scoop out the pulp and blend it with basic filling ingredients (as in basic recipe). Flavour with a little curry powder and 3 Tbs yoghurt. Stuff each half of aubergine with this filling.

B Bake aubergine for 20 mins at 400 °F/200 °C/Gas Mark 6. Scoop out pulp and cream it in a bowl with half its own weight of oil and yoghurt, and a little lemon juice. Flavour with chopped garlic. Season to taste, and serve as a filling for pancakes.

C Serrate the aubergines with a fork or insert prongs of fork and prick all over. Soak in salt, wash and dry, then pass in seasoned flour. Deep fry in oil for 1 minute. Drain, season, and serve with a wedge of lemon.

Chef's Tips

- soaking in salt extracts the bitter juice from the aubergine, and is well worth the extra time.
- A quicker way is to wash the sliced aubergines in water with a little vinegar.
- aubergine slices, hot or cold, can be served as a delicious snack to go with drinks.

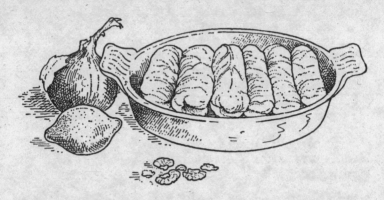

42

Vine Leaves stuffed with Rice and Dried Fruit

Ingredients

vine leaves
  16 — canned or fresh
Filling:
  rice (5oz/150g) uncooked
    long-grain
  sultanas (2oz/50g)
  onion (1oz/25g) grated
  walnuts (2oz/50g) shelled
  chicken stock
    (2 pints/1200ml)
  lemon juice and rind of 1
  salt to taste
  white pepper to taste
  dill, chopped, to taste

Preparation time 30 mins **Cooking time** 50 mins
Portions 6 **Calories per portion** 140

Method

1 If the vine leaves are fresh, blanch them in salted water for 4 mins. If canned this need not be done.
2 Boil the rice for no more than 12 mins in 3 cups of water. Drain and cool.
3 Scald sultanas for 2 mins, and then blend with them the rest of the filling ingredients.
4 Fill each leaf, and roll to a cigar shape. Place them in a shallow ovenware dish and cover with stock. Add lemon juice, grated rind and seasoning.
5 Cover with a lid and bake for 35 mins in a moderate oven.

Variations

A Vine leaves can be replaced with medium sized cabbage leves. Proceed as in the basic recipe folding into squares 2" × 2" (5cm × 5cm).
B The stuffing or filling can be modified by adding a little raw minced meat or fish to the rice.
C Try cooking the stuffed vine leaves in fruit juices rather than chicken stock, or alternatively some wine.

Chef's Tips

- it's important to remember in this recipe that the rice should not be over-cooked before you start.
- serve the dolmas (vine leaves) with a lemon sauce made with the liquid from the casserole put in a saucepan with egg yolks and lemon juice, thickened with potato farina (instant mash)
- dolmas will keep frozen in their stock, but preferably make the sauce fresh. If you intend to freeze the sauce you must use cornflour not instant potato powder.
- for ½ pint/300 ml of lemon sauce mix 1 egg yolk, 2 tsp cornflour (or instant potato powder) add 2 Tbs water in a cup. Mix well. Boil stock from casserole (½ pint/300ml) in a saucepan and gently stir in the egg mixture until it thickens. Then add grated rind and juice of ½ lemon.

43

Peppers stuffed with Minced Beef, Onions and Mushrooms

Ingredients

green peppers 8 medium
Stuffing:
   beef (12oz/350g) minced
   egg 1
   garlic 1 clove chopped
   tomato purée (2oz/50g)
   onions (4oz/100g)
     chopped
   mushrooms (4oz/100g)
     chopped
   salt and **pepper**
   yoghurt (4fl oz/100ml)
   bread crumbs (4oz/100g)
   oil for frying

Preparation time 15 mins   **Cooking time** 75 mins
Portions 8   **Calories per portion** 225

Method

1 Cut the head off each pepper and put to one side. Deseed them.
2 Parboil the peppers for 5 mins in salted water, and put to one side.
3 Sauté minced beef with onions until brown. Add a little water and boil till tender — 20 mins. Season to taste.
4 Blend together tomato purée, yoghurt, egg, mushrooms and crumbs. Add cooked meat and onions. Season to taste.
5 Fill the peppers with the mixture, and when full replace the cap of each pepper.
6 Arrange stuffed peppers in a shallow oven dish. Half fill the dish with stock or water (about half way up the sides of the peppers). Cover with greased paper, and bake for 45 mins.
7 Serve.

Variations

A Use tomatoes instead of peppers. They need to be large. Proceed as in the basic recipe, without parboiling tomatoes and bake for only 15 minutes instead of 45 mins.
B Stuff the mixture into 8 parboiled (for about 10 mins) cabbage leaves. Wrap the leaves into balls, and place them tightly together in a shallow dish half-filled with stock or water. Brush the top with oil and season. Bake for 45 mins. Serve hot or cold with a tomato sauce.
C Clean, wash and peel eight courgettes. Make a hole at one end, and remove seeds and pulp to form a hollow. Fill with the stuffing mixture. Proceed as in basic recipe.

Chef's Tips

● when stuffing peppers it is not necessary to parboil them first.
● red peppers have a better flavour than green.
● instead of crumbs used in a stuffing you can always substitute cooked rice.
● a meat-based stuffing can often be varied by substituting fish or eggs.

44

Stuffed Mushrooms
With various cheesy fillings

Ingredients

field mushrooms (1 lb/450g)
  wild not cultivated
flour (2oz/50g) seasoned
garlic 2 cloves chopped
Filling:
  onions (1oz/25g) chopped
  parsley 1 Tbs chopped
Yeast batter:
  flour (4oz/100g)
  egg 1
  yeast 1 tsp
  water (½pt/300ml)
  salt a pinch

Preparation time 10 mins　**Fermentation time** 1 hour
  Cooking time 1½ mins
Portions 4　**Calories per portion** 130

Method

1 Remove stalks from the mushrooms, wash and drain well. Chop the stalks keeping caps whole.
2 Pass the caps in seasoned flour, flavoured with chopped garlic.
3 Combine cheese with onions, parsley and chopped stalks.
4 Spread cheese mixture on the inside of the mushroom caps.
5 Combine egg and water. Crumble yeast and mix well. Add flour. Leave to ferment at room temperature for 1 hour.
6 Heat oil in a pan. Dip mushrooms in yeast batter, and then deep fry in very hot fat for 1½ minutes.
7 Drain well and serve on cocktail sticks.

Variations

A Sandwich cheese mixture with 2 mushroom caps and proceed as before.
B Pass mushrooms in flour, then in beaten egg only. Roll in bread crumbs, mixed with a little grated cheese. Deep fry until golden brown.
C Make a Welsh rarebit mixture. Combine grated cheese (4oz/100g) with 1 egg yolk, 1 tsp Worcestershire sauce, and 1 tsp mustard. Spread this on the inside of the mushrooms. Brown under the grill, until cheese is golden.

Chef's Tips

- only half cook the mushrooms. They taste much better and hold their shape better.
- field mushrooms or larger frying mushrooms have a stronger flavour than the white mushrooms usually bought in supermarkets.
- do not use tinned mushrooms for this sort of dish.
- if mushrooms are fresh and well-washed there is no need to peel. If the very end of the stalk is removed the rest of the stalk can be chopped up and used as filling.

45

Spaghetti Napolitaine
A traditional Italian tomato sauce and pasta dish.

Ingredients

spaghetti (8oz/225g)
butter (1oz/25g)
salt ½ Tbs
cheese (2oz/50g) — cheddar,
    parmesan, gruyere grated
salt and pepper to taste
oil 1 tsp
water 2 pints/1200ml
Sauce:
    oil (2fl oz/50ml) 4 Tbs
    onions (5oz/150g)
       chopped

flour (1½oz/35g)
tomato purée (2oz/50g)
tomatoes 4 (8oz/225g)
    fresh, chopped
garlic 1 clove crushed
salt 1 tsp
black pepper 1 tsp
sugar 1 tsp
oregano a pinch
water or stock
    (½ pint/300ml)

Preparation time 15 mins   **Cooking time** 25 mins
Portions 4   **Calories per portion** 580

Method

1 Bring salted water to boil and add 1 tsp oil.
2 Coil spaghetti in the saucepan without breaking, and cook
   for 12-15 minutes, depending on the thickness of
   spaghetti.

3 Drain. Blend butter, grated cheese, salt and pepper, and place in a large shallow dish.

4 Make the sauce while spaghetti is cooking. Heat the oil and sauté the onions and garlic without browning too much. Add flour and cook for 2 mins stirring all the time. Blend in the tomato purée, chopped tomatoes, seasoning and water or stock.

5 Simmer for 12 minutes until sauce is quite thick. Adjust seasoning to taste.

6 Serve spaghetti and sauce together or separately.

Variations

A Try a minced meat sauce — a bolognaise. Simply brown 4oz/100g minced meat in a pan, and then add this meat to the tomato sauce.

B Use a little carrot and celery in the sauce to alter the flavour: about 2oz/50g of each.

C Add to tomatoes same amount (8oz/225g) of red peppers or sliced olives to make a more piquant sauce.

Chef's Tips

- if fresh tomatoes are not available, double the quantity of tomato purée or use tinned tomatoes.
- a better sauce is made by using chicken stock instead of water; for this you can add a stock cube. A beef stock cube will result in a richer, meatier flavour.
- try adding some wine or sherry to the sauce for a richer flavour.
- always leave yourself time to reduce the sauce so it is thick enough.
- pasta absorbs 2.3 times its own weight in water, so multiply the weight of pasta used by at least 4 times the *quantity* of water (225g pasta = 1000-1200ml water) when boiling pasta

Lasagne

A basic recipe for making your own pasta.

Ingredients

flour (½lb/225g) bread
   variety
eggs 2
egg yolk 1
oil 1 Tbs vegetable
salt ½ tsp
semolina a handful of raw

Preparation time 30 mins plus 30 mins resting   **Cooking time** 8 mins
Portions 4   **Calories per portion** 275

Method

1 Sift flour and salt.
2 Combine eggs, yolk and oil, and blend into flour. Knead to a dough.
3 Rest for 30 mins.
4 To cut to shape, dust pastry board with flour to prevent sticking.

5 Roll mixture to an oblong sausage ⅛th inch (3mm) thick. Fold in four, and then cut into ½ inch (12mm) ribbons.
6 Line a tray with a cloth, and dust with raw semolina to prevent any sticking. Place ribbons on tray.
7 Dry the ribbons on top of the cooker, and when they are brittle they are ready to be cooked.
8 Boil for 6-8 minutes in salted water.
9 Serve with grated cheese and a pat of butter.

Variations

A The pasta can be coloured green, by using spinach juice, or pink by using tomato juice. Simply add a touch more flour to make sure the consistency is right.
B The same pasta can be used for ravioli and other fillings can be used.
C The freshly made pasta can be made with a variety of sauces — Bolognaise, Milanaise or Napolitaine.

Chef's Tips

- remember whether ready made or home made, pasta should not be overcooked.
- to prevent pasta sticking add 1 Tbs oil to the boiling water.
- try and serve immediately the pasta is cooked. However, pasta can be refrigerated when almost cooked, then placed in boiling water later for a short while until ready to be served.
- a medium-sized egg should weigh 2oz/50g (out of shell).

47

Ravioli

An easy way to make a more complicated Italian pasta dish.

Ingredients

pasta as made in Lasagne
   recipe (12oz/350g) pre-
   cooked weight
Filling
   beef raw minced
     (6oz/175g) or a mixture of
     beef and pork

spinach (2oz/50g) cooked,
chopped and well drained.
salt, pepper, nutmeg and
   ground oregano a pinch
   of each
egg 1 (to bind mixture)

Preparation time 45 mins   **Cooking time** 15 mins
  Resting time 1 hour
Portions 4   **Calories per portion** 180-200

Method

1 First prepare pasta as in Lasagne recipe. Rest for 30
  minutes.
2 For filling combine all ingredients in a bowl.
3 To shape the ravioli, dust a pastry board with flour or raw
  semolina to stop pasta sticking. Roll pasta to ⅛ inch (3mm)
  thickness. Divide the pasta into two equal pieces — one
  for the base, and one for the top. Rest for 30 mins.

4 Use a ruler to mark out one inch (25mm) squares on both pieces of pasta.
5 In the centre of each square place a small amount of the filling mixture, on one piece of pasta only.
6 Wet the pasta around the meat. Place the second piece of pasta on top, covering the meat squares.
7 Use a small inverted pastry cutter or the blunt edge of a knife to press the edges of each square together, and to seal the two pasta pieces.
8 Then cut the squares, and make sure each ravioli piece is properly sealed.
9 Poach in a shallow tray half filled with salted water for 10-15 minutes.

Variations

A Try chicken or any other minced liver in the filling, in the same quantity as the minced beef.
B Try using raw white fish instead of meat.
C For a vegetarian dish you can used nuts instead of meat (the same quantity) and blend in some peas and chopped spinach.
D For an alternative filling combine cream cheese (2oz/50g), the yolk of one egg, 1 Tbs flour, some grated lemon rind, a pinch of salt and 2 tsp sugar. When poached, as in the basic recipe, soak in 2 cups (275ml) water. Drain and serve in sauce.

Chef's Tips

• to prevent the ravioli sticking together while cooking, use a large saucepan, and when putting them in don't put too many in one place and make sure first that the water is boiling.
• the most common sauce to use with ravioli is tomato (see spaghetti recipe), but use your imagination and try other variations. Add 50 calories per portion for a tomato sauce.
• leave ravioli in sauce overnight in refrigerator. When reheated in oven in a shallow dish they will be more tender.
• to get 2oz/50g cooked, drained spinach use 8oz/225g raw spinach

111

48

Macaroni fritters

A hot, filling and inexpensive dish

Ingredients

macaroni (4oz/100g) cooked
 cut in 1 inch/25mm
 sections
white sauce (4fl oz/100ml)
 (see *Variations on a
 Recipe by the same
 authors*)
eggs 2 beaten medium
ham (2oz/50g) diced cooked
gherkin 1 chopped
salt and **pepper**
flour for dusting
oil for frying

Preparation time 10 mins   **Frying time** 5 mins
 Chilling time 1 hour
Portions 16 fritters (1oz/25g each)   **Calories per portion** 250
 per fritter

Method

1 Reheat (or make fresh) white sauce and add gherkins, macaroni, ham, and season to taste. Boil 5 mins. Remove from heat.
2 Blend the two beaten eggs into the hot mixture — and chill in a greased oblong tray (about 2 ins deep and 8 by 4 inches wide) for about 1 hour.
3 When cold and solidified cut the mixture into squares, say 2 ins by 2 ins, pass in flour and shallow fry.
4 Serve.

Variations

A Use diced chicken instead of ham, and add some sliced mushrooms to the mixture.
B Use flaked cooked haddock, or prawns, instead of the ham.
C Add 2oz/50g sweet corn to the mixture, together with 1 sliced green chilli and some diced corned beef or sliced cooked sausage.
D Place mixture into flour, beaten egg and breadcrumbs and deep fry.

Chef's Tips

● pasta when cooked and cooled in white sauce tends to solidify. It can therefore be cut into attractive shapes before cooking.
● when making macaroni or pasta fritters, blend the cooked pasta with a white sauce to which has been added 2 raw eggs per pint of white sauce. This will enrich the meal nutritionally.
● this dish is excellent as a snack too.
● the calorie content of fried food is based on the amount of oil retained, which depends on the extent of absorption by the ingredients — on average it is between 10-15% of the fat used

49

Macaroni with Walnuts and Yoghurt

Baked pasta with vegetarian or meat sauces, eaten hot or cold

Ingredients

macaroni (8oz/225g)
cream (6fl oz/175ml) double
yoghurt (3oz/75g)
walnuts (5oz/150g) ground
   or chopped
egg yolks 3
tomatoes (10oz/275g)
   6 medium fresh
butter (2oz/50g)
flour (2oz/50g)
cheese (2oz/50g) cheddar
   grated
salt and pepper
garlic 1 clove
nutmeg ground, a pinch

Preparation time 15 mins   **Cooking time** 25 mins
Portions 6   **Calories per portion** 590

Method

1 Boil macaroni in salted water for 15 minutes. Refresh and drain.
2 Melt the butter in a pan, add flour and stir until a sandy texture; gradually add cream, and yoghurt and then the egg yolks. Season with salt and pepper, grated nutmeg and crushed garlic.
3 Blend the sauce with the macaroni, but save some of the sauce for the topping.
4 Place macaroni in a shallow dish. Cover with the rest of the sauce. Sprinkle grated cheese and chopped walnuts.
5 Bake in the oven until brown.
6 Brush the surface with melted butter, and decorate with slices of tomato.
7 Serve cold or reheat under the grill.

Variations

A Add a little diced chicken or ham to the sauce.
B Add some loose corn to the sauce, or peas or beans.
C Instead of topping with tomatoes, try sliced fried aubergines or sliced cooked marrow or peeled avocado pear.

Chef's Tips

- the sauce can be made simpler by using milk rather than cream (and cheaper).
- the best cheeses to use in order of flavour are Gruyére, Parmesan, Gouda, Edam, Cheddar.
- for economy, an equal quantity of crushed salted peanuts and breadcrumbs can be blended with the grated cheese.
- cooked macaroni bound in thick white sauce can be used as a topping like mashed potato in shepherd's pie.
- or it can be used as a base, with a lighter topping such as fish or breast of chicken

115

50

Stuffed Pancakes
Pancakes filled with cheese and nuts, or meat

Ingredients

Batter:
  egg 1
  flour (4oz/100g) plain
  milk (½ pint/300ml)
  parsley chopped 1 Tbs
    fresh
  salt and pepper
  cheese grated 1 Tbs
    cheddar
  oil 2 Tbs (frying)
Filling:
  cottage or cream cheese
    (4oz/100g)
  garlic 1 chopped clove
  chives 1 Tbs chopped fresh
  egg 1 beaten

walnuts chopped
  (3oz/75g)
aubergine chopped and
  peeled (3oz/75g)
salt and pepper
chilli pepper 1 pinch

Preparation time 45 mins   Cooking time 5 mins
Portions 4   Calories per portion 425

Method

1 Beat egg and blend with milk, salt, pepper, chopped parsley and grated cheese. Mix in flour to produce a smooth batter. Rest for 30 mins.
2 Heat a little oil in a pan and cover bottom of pan thinly with batter. Cook pancakes on both sides. Leave on a tray to cool.
3 Combine all the filling ingredients into a smooth paste, and divide it to fill each pancake. Roll pancakes into cigar shapes.
4 Pass in flour and beaten egg and deep fry in oil for 1 min until golden.
5 Drain and serve with a sprinkling of salt and paprika.

Variations

A Fill pancakes with cooked minced beef. Coat with cheese sauce and sprinkle on grated cheese. Brown in oven.
B Add diced ham to mixture. After passing pancakes in flour and beaten egg, pass in dessicated coconut before frying.
C Add diced cooked turkey, sweet corn and red peppers to basic mixture. Add a good pinch of chilli pepper. Pass in flour, beaten egg and breadcrumbs before frying. Serve with a peppery tomato sauce.

Chef's Tips

- make sure the pancakes are small and thin (about 6'' in diameter) — remember it's just a wrapping for the filling.
- pancakes can be made in advance. They can be piled up and kept in refrigerator until needed, when they can be deep fried at the last minute.
- whole wheat flour can be added to white flour if desired.
- batter for pancakes can be made lighter by using a little baking powder or fresh yeast.

51

Tortillas

Corn pancakes, Mexican style, with different fillings

Ingredients

cornmeal (10oz/275g)
wheat flour(2oz/50g)
salt 1 tsp
water (6 fl oz/200ml)

Preparation time 25 mins   **Cooking time** 10 mins
Portions 4   **Calories per portion** 300

Method

1 Blend all ingredients to form a stiffish dough. Mould into a ball and rest for 15 minutes.
2 Divide the dough into small dumplings the size of an egg. Place one at a time between two sheets of polythene and roll to a thick pancake about 5 ins in diameter.
3 Bake on greased trays at a high heat (400 °F/200 °C/Gas Mark 6) until the pancakes begin to blister.
4 Stack the tortillas inside a napkin to keep warm. Sprinkle with salt and serve.

Variations

A Transform the tortilla pancakes into enchilladas — stuffed pancakes. After cooking the pancakes stuff with a mixture of cooked minced beef (8oz/225g), cooked chopped onions (2oz/50g), tomato purée (1oz/25g), grated cheese (1oz/25g), and a pinch of chilli pepper. To make this mixture blend all the ingredients together, add a cup of water (¼ pint/150ml) and simmer for 15 minutes until the mixture thickens. Then stuff the tortillas, and serve with a tomato sauce (see spaghetti recipe) or add one chilli pepper to the sauce to spice it up.

B For a softer tortilla, replace the water with milk or cream.

C Transform this dish into a pudding by serving tortillas with honey or golden syrup.

Chef's Tips

- cornmeal is maize semolina, and is available in most supermarkets.
- mash up a can of baked beans — with sauce — and use as a filling for tortilla. Hot it up with tabasco or chilli sauce.
- eat with salads — avocado pear and tomatoes — cut up and made into a sandwich.
- tortillas can be made in advance and kept in the fridge in greaseproof paper for a week. To reheat brush with a little butter and place in very hot oven for 3-4 mins (or 1 min under the grill like toast).

52

Quichette Lorraine

Variations on delicious hot individual savoury flans

Ingredients

Pastry:
    flour (½lb/225g) plain
    margarine (4oz/100g)
    cheese 1 Tbs cheddar
      grated (or any other
      hard cheese)
    egg 1
    butter (2oz/50g)

Filling:
    cream (5fl oz/150ml)
      single
    eggs 2
    salt and **pepper**
    cheese 1 Tbs cheddar
      grated
    paprika and **grated**
      nutmeg pinch of each

Preparation time 1½ hours   **Cooking time** 25 mins
Portions 10   **Calories per portion** 300

Method

1 Pastry: grease well with unmelted soft vegetable fat (or lard) 10 small tartlet moulds 3 inches in diameter (8cm).
2 Rub flour and margarine into a crumbly consistency.
3 Beat egg and grated cheese, and blend into dough mixture until stiff. Roll into a ball and rest for 30 mins.
4 Roll to a thickness of one eighth of an inch (3mm), and

with a 3½ inch (10cm) cutter make as many rounds as possible.

5 Line the moulds with pastry, then prick the pastry with a fork.

6 Brush the inside of the pastry with a little melted butter. This will prevent filling making pastry soggy.

7 Placing on baking sheet and rest for ½ hour in refrigerator.

8 **Filling:** beat eggs with cheese and seasoning. Blend in single cream and pour mixture into each mould until about two thirds full.

9 Bake at 400 °F/200 °C/Gas Mark 6 for 12-15 mins. Remove from oven and fill moulds to the top and rebake for another 10 mins.

10 Cool before removing quichettes from moulds.

Variations

A To basic filling add 2oz (50g) each of sliced mushrooms, sliced ham and turkey, chopped cooked red pepper and sweet corn.

B Sweat ½lb/240g sliced onions in butter until soft but not brown. Add to filling mixture.

C Use the onions, but add sliced olives, chopped anchovy fillets, chopped parsley and flavour with a clove of finely chopped garlic and the pulp of a tomato and shredded cooked spinach or shredded raw lettuce.

Chef's Tips

- sprinkle on grated parmesan cheese before baking to improve flavour.
- if you use bacon in the preparation of this dish, use unsalted streaky rather than back, and scald the bacon first with boiling water, then cool it before using.
- milk can be substituted for cream, and any kind of vegetables can be used instead of meat: peas, corn, carrots, beans, etc.
- if raw onions are used (see **Variation B**) you will get a stronger flavour.
- all moulds should be greased with **unmelted** fat or butter — this helps the pastry not to stick to the mould.

53

Moules Marinière

Mussels in white wine

Ingredients

mussels (4 pints/2 litres)
butter (1oz/25g)
onions (2oz/50g) chopped
dry white wine
    (½ pint/300ml)
white vinegar 1 Tbs
bay leaf 1
thyme 1 sprig
pepper black or white
    a pinch
parsley 2 Tbs chopped fresh

Preparation time 15 mins   Cooking time 7 mins
Portions 4   Calories per portion 180

Method

1 Scrub and scrape mussels and remove any seaweed. Wash
   in plenty of running cold water.
2 Heat butter and gently sauté onions for 1 minute.

3 Stir in wine, add all herbs except parsley and pepper. Then add mussels.

4 Cover with a lid, bring to boil for 6 mins.

5 Sprinkle chopped parsley and pepper before serving.

Variations

A After the mussels are cooked, strain sauce into a small saucepan. Blend 2 egg yolks and ¼ pint/150ml cream in a bowl. Add mussel juice. Reheat in saucepan, and then pour over mussels.

B Same as the basic recipe, but add 5oz/150g chopped tomatoes as well as a sprig of tarragon.

C Use red wine or cider instead of white wine.

Chef's Tips

- if after 6 minutes of cooking there are mussels which haven't opened: **throw them away: they are bad.**
- Mussels can be used as a garnish for sea-food cocktails.
- raw mussels can be grilled in their opened shells. Before cooking, open the shell and fill with a butter to which some crushed garlic and chopped parsley has been added. Grill or bake for 5 minutes.

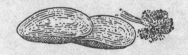

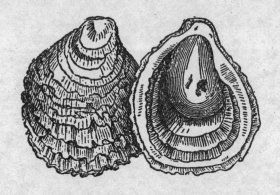

54

Grilled Oysters with Bacon

Ingredients

oysters 8 raw
bacon 4 rashers of lean
   smoked, streaky or back
bread 2 slices toasted and
   cut into four fingers each
butter
cayenne pepper a pinch

Preparation time 5 mins (plus desalting)
   Cooking time 6 mins
Portions 4   **Calories per portion** 475

Method

1 Desalt bacon rashers for half an hour in cold water. Wipe
  and dry.
2 Make toast.
3 Remove rind, flatten each rasher, and cut in 2 pieces.

4 Wrap each oyster with a piece of bacon. Roll tightly and secure with a cocktail stick.
5 Brush with melted butter and grill for just under a minute.
6 Place on toast fingers, dust with cayenne pepper and serve.

Variations

A Instead of oysters, raw scallops or scampi can be used. In these instances also wrap in bacon and cook until crisp.
B Small fish fillets, cut 2 inches long, can also be wrapped in rashers of bacon. Use lemon juice and brush with a little oil during grilling.
C Take some pineapple cubes, and wrap each cube together with a prawn inside a rasher of bacon. When grilled, sprinkle with a little Worcestershire sauce.
D Wrap chicken livers in bacon, or stoned prunes stuffed with mango chutney.
E Place each raw oyster in the bottom part of its shell, sprinkle on grated cheese, place under the grill for about 1 min.

Chef's Tips

- in all these recipes serve with cucumber slices and wedges of lemon or other crudités.
- oysters should be eaten from September to April (each month with the letter 'r' in it.)
- when not in season use canned, smoked oysters.

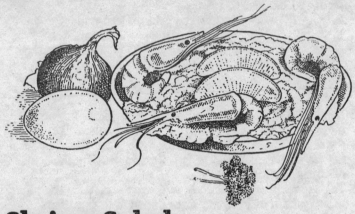

55

Shrimp Salad

Shrimps and salad with piquant dressing

Ingredients

shrimps or prawns
(1½ lbs/675g) peeled and
preboiled or frozen
Sauce:
  oil (4fl oz/100ml)
  wine vinegar (2fl oz/50ml)
  eggs 2 hard boiled
  onions (2oz/50g) chopped
  peppers (2oz/50g)
    chopped
  capers (½oz/15g) chopped
  parsley 1 Tbs chopped
  tomato ketchup
    (1fl oz/25ml)
  anchovy (1oz/25g)
    chopped

white sauce (4fl oz/100ml)
English mustard 1 tsp
salt and **pepper** to taste
lettuce 6 leaves for garnish
grapefruit 2 for garnish

Preparation time 40 mins   **Cooking time** 10 mins
Portions 6 **Calories per portion** 400

Method

1 Chop the hard-boiled eggs and sieve to a paste.
2 Combine all the ingredients of the sauce.
3 Blend in the peeled shrimps or prawns.
4 Chill for 30 minutes.
5 Serve on lettuce leaves with grapefruit segements for decoration.

Variations

A Frozen scampi can be used as an alternative, and there's no need to thaw them out. Place them in ¼ pint/150ml water, and the same quantity of white wine. Add 2 slices of onion and a sprig of thyme, bring to boil then simmer for 8 minutes. Allow to cool, and when cold pour on sauce.

B As prawns are fairly expensive, combine half the quantity of white fish, flaked or cut into small pieces.

C A simpler way to produce a similar sauce is to make a mayonnaise first or use ready-made mayonnaise. Then add 1 tsp each of onions, gherkins, parsley and chopped egg. Anchovy essence can be used instead of anchovy fillet, and tomato purée instead of chopped tomatoes or ketchup.

Chef's Tips

● presentation of this dish can be improved by shredding the lettuce leaves, and arranging them in a glass. Put in shrimps or prawns, and then add sauce.

● the prawns can be mixed with rice or potato salad.

● to make your own mayonnaise or salad dressing: heat 1oz/25g of margarine, add 1oz/25g flour, cook for 1 min without colouring; gradually add 1 cup hot water, whisking to a smooth paste; thin down with 5fl oz/150ml single cream or yoghurt to produce the consistency of a thick sauce; add 1 tsp prepared English mustard, salt and pepper to taste and finally 2 tsp vinegar or lemon juice. When cold whisk in 1 Tbs oil. Keep in fridge.

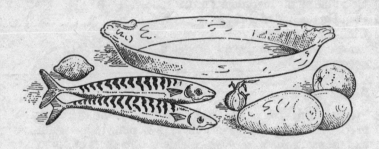

56

Mackerel and Fruit Salad
Smoked mackerel and tropical fruits

Ingredients

smoked mackerel 2 small
   (1 lb/450g) filleted
lemon juice of 1
orange juice of 1
salt and **pepper**
ginger 1 small piece of fresh
onion 1 small chopped
white vinegar 1 Tbs
honey 1 tsp
pawpaw 2 medium size
Garnish:
   lettuce leaves
   parsley
   coriander leaves
   black olives 6

Preparation time 15 mins
Portions 4   **Calories per portion** 285

Method

1 Skin the smoked mackerel fillets and cut in small pieces. Place in a shallow dish together with orange and lemon juice, chopped onion, all the seasoning, and the honey and vinegar.
2 Cut the pawpaw in 2 halves lengthways. Scoop out the seeds in the centre and fill with fish mixture.
3 Arrange garnish and mackerel-filled pawpaw on a plate and serve.

Variations

A Instead of pawpaw use avocado pears — allow half per person.
B The mackerel can be replaced by other similar fish — herring, trout or mullet.
C Instead of pawpaw or avocado, scoop out a cucumber and fill the cavity with the fish. In this case cover with a pineapple dressing (6 Tbs of cream flavoured with a little pineapple juice).
D Marinaded kipper fillets are also an excellent filling for pawpaw. Simply soak the kippers in white vinegar with a pickling mixture: coriander seeds, chilli pepper, garlic, peppercorns, onion and carrot for 2 days. Drain, then dice the fillets and fill pawpaw as in the basic recipe.

Chef's Tips

• use a little plain yoghurt or French mayonnaise as a dressing.
• a creamy horseradish dressing will also go well with this dish.
• fresh mackerel fillets can also be used: wash and rinse, then bake for 25 mins at 180 °C/350 °F/Gas Mark 4; leave fish in liquid until cold. Then peel off skin and cut flesh into small pieces. Strain the liquid and add chopped onions (as in basic recipe) to fish. Continue as in recipe.
• a purée of gooseberry and rhubarb, sweetened to taste, can also be served as a garnish.

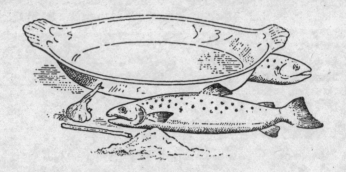

57

Barbecued Trout Fillets

Marinaded and baked in a spicy sauce

Ingredients

trout filleted (4 medium
   8oz/225g each)
Marinade:
   soya sauce 1 Tbs
   garlic 1 clove chopped
   fresh ginger 1 small piece
   brown sugar 1 tsp

malt vinegar 1 Tbs
pineapple juice 1 cup
(5fl oz/150ml)
flour (2oz/50g) seasoned
oil for shallow frying
parsley 1 Tbs

Preparation time 40 mins   Cooking time 10 mins
Portions 4   Calories per portion 315

Method

1 Liquidise all ingredients of the marinade.
2 Soak fish fillets in it for 30 mins.
3 Drain and pass fish in flour.
4 Heat oil in a pan, and shallow fry fish in it for 6 mins.
5 Transfer fish onto a serving dish.
6 Boil marinade for 3 minutes, and pour sauce over fish.
7 Sprinkle chopped parsley and serve.

Variations

A Change the marinade:

white vinegar 1 Tbs   **tarragon** 1 sprig of, chopped
tomato juice (¼ pint/150ml)   **salt** and **pepper**
garlic 2 cloves

Liquidise these ingredients, and marinade fish as in the basic recipe. Then cook as before.

B Another marinade could be:

dill 1 tsp
white vinegar (4fl oz/100ml)
honey 1 Tbs
yoghurt ½ cup

Combine ingredients. Marinade fish for 30 minutes. Place fish in shallow dish, cover with marinade. Bake for 15-20 minutes at 180 °C/350 °F/Gas Mark 4. Cool, and serve with, for example, potato salad.

C Sweet and sour marinade:

onion 1 sliced thinly   **garlic** 1 clove chopped
carrot 1 sliced thinly   **water** (¼ pint/150ml)
pickled cucumber 1 chopped   **white vinegar** 4 Tbs
white wine (¼ pint/150ml)   **bay leaf** 1
chilli pepper 1 sliced thinly   **thyme** sprig of
tomato purée (2oz/50g)   **salt** and **pepper**

Place fish in a shallow dish; cover with marinade and soak for 24 hours refrigerated. Bake for 8 minutes in the same marinade at 180 °C/350 °F/Gas Mark 4.

Chef's Tips

- what is applicable for trout is equally applicable to many other oily fish, such as mackerel, salmon, sea trout, haddock, herrings, kippers or bloaters.
- all oily fish require an accidulant, which can be provided by stock to which vinegar has been added. German-style would involve cooking the fish in sour cream. Such fish should first be salted and pickled in white vinegar for 24 hours, drained and reheated for 5 mins in sour cream. Eat hot or cold.

58

Fish Cakes
A hot or cold starter

Ingredients

minced fish (1 lb/450g) raw
— white fish, trout or
salmon, cod or haddock
onions (1oz/25g) grated
rice (4oz/100g)
salt and **white pepper**
lemon juice and grated rind
of 1
sugar 1 tsp white
chicken stock cube ½
parsley 1 Tbs chopped
oil (2fl oz/50ml) for frying
seasoned flour (2oz/50g)
egg 1 raw

Preparation time 20 mins   **Cooking time** 5 mins
Portions 6   **Calories per portion** 250

Method

1 Boil the rice for 20 mins then drain.
2 Combine fish, rice and onions and egg with the seasoning
  and parsley. Blend to a firm paste.
3 Divide into scone-like cakes.
4 Pass in seasoned flour and flatten as thin as possible (to ½
  inch high/2½ inch in diameter).
5 Heat oil in a frying pan.
6 Shallow-fry the fish cakes on both sides for 4 minutes.
7 Serve with lemon juice and grated lemon rind.

Variations

A Instead of cooked rice use 4oz/100g cold mashed potatoes
  and 1 raw egg. Blend with fish and other ingredients then
  shape mixture into balls and flatten like a hamburger. Try
  coating with brown bread crumbs and flaked almonds or
  with matzo meal before shallow frying.
B Instead of rice, combine 2oz/50g breadcrumbs and 1
  chopped hard-boiled egg and 1oz/25g of chopped
  walnuts. Mix with fish and proceed as in the basic recipe.
C If preferred you can bake the fish on shallow trays in the
  oven instead of frying. If you do this, add a little stock to
  prevent the fish cakes drying out.

Chef's Tips

● remember to serve with a wedge of lemon, or a
  mayonnaise with chopped mint, or a cucumber and
  yoghurt sauce (made with 4oz/100g yoghurt, 2oz/50g
  cucumber, a clove of garlic and some parsley all liquidised
  together).
● try adding some cod's roe to minced fish to enhance the
  flavour, as well as a clove of garlic (finely chopped).
● for more protein increase the ratio of fish to rice; to keep
  the cost of the dish down reverse the ratio.

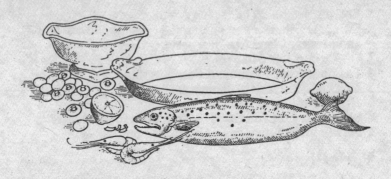

59

Salmon and Prawn in puff pastry with a Mushroom Sauce

Ingredients

smoked salmon (4oz/100g) thinly sliced
puff pastry (1 lb/450g) — frozen will do
prawns (4oz/100g) peeled
parsley 1 Tbs chopped
lemon 1 sliced
dill 1 sprig
mushroom sauce:
  white sauce (¼ pint/150ml) thick
  button mushrooms 1 cup (4oz/100g)

cheese (2oz/50g), cheddar or parmesan grated
anchovy essence 1 Tbs
paprika a pinch
salt and **pepper**
lemon juice of half
salmon filling:
  prawns (4oz/100g) peeled
  mayonnaise (¼ pint/150ml)
  smoked salmon (4oz/100g) chopped trimmings

Preparation time 40 mins **Cooking time** 30 mins Cooling time 1 hour
Portions 8 **Calories per portion** 300

Method

1 Preheat the oven to 200 °C/400 °F/Gas Mark 6.
2 Roll out the thawed pastry to a thickness of ⅛ inch/4mm. Cut out three circles 8 inches(20cm in diameter).
3 Place the pastry circles on a greased baking tray, and prick the pastry with a fork. Bake for 15 minutes.
4 While the pastry is baking prepare the fillings. Heat the white sauce and stir in chopped mushrooms, anchovy essence and paprika. Simmer for 5 mins, then season. Add the lemon juice, and cool a little before adding the grated cheese.
5 Blend the prawns with 4fl oz/100ml mayonnaise. Stir in the chopped smoked salmon, making sure all skin and bones have been removed.
6 When the pastry is cooked and has cooled, place one circle on a large round plate, and generously spread over the mushroom sauce. Top with another pastry circle, and cover with most of the smoked salmon mixture. Place the third pastry slice on top and cover with the remaining mayonnaise.
7 Roll up the smoked salmon slices and fill with the remaining smoked salmon mixture. Arrange these rolls on top of the pastry.
8 Decorate with peeled prawns and sprinkle on herbs. Arrange lemon slices and chill for 30 minutes before serving.

Variations

A Instead of prawns, use crab, lobster or scampi in the same quantities.
B Instead of smoked salmon use smoked kippers or smoked trout.
C Instead of mushroom filling, replace with mayonnaise mixed with chopped olives.

Chef's Tips

- the shape of the finished dish can be changed to be rectangular or square.
- this can also be made using short pastry. Or try the fish wrapped in pancakes.

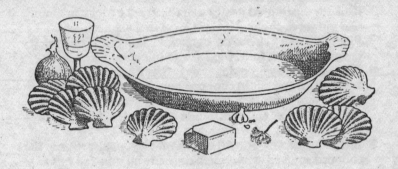

60

Coquille St. Jacques
Scallops poached in white wine with a cheesy sauce

Ingredients

scallops 8 (1 lb/450g)
white wine (¼ pint/150ml)
Sauce:
  butter (2oz/50g)
  onions (2oz/50g) chopped
  white mushrooms
    (2oz/50g) sliced
  flour (1 oz/25g)
  cream (2fl oz/50ml)
  lemon juice of half
  salt 3 pinches
  pepper 1 pinch
  ground nutmeg 1 pinch
  cheese (2oz/50g) grated
  potato (½ lb/225g)

Preparation time 25 mins   **Cooking time** 40 mins
Portions 4 (2 scallops per person per deep shell)   **Calories**
  per portion 400

Method

1 Boil potatoes for mashing.
2 Wash scallops well in plenty of water. Remove beard. Keep only the white meat and orange roe.
3 Cover in water and wine, and poach for 5-8 minutes. Keep the juice.
4 Remove scallops from liquid, and then strain liquid through a fine sieve.
5 Pipe a border of mashed potato round the shell to hold the sauce. Dry the potato in the oven for 10 minutes.
6 Place 2 cooked scallops in each shell.
7 For the sauce, heat butter in a pan and gently sauté the onions for 2 minutes. Add the mushrooms. Stir and cook for a further 30 secs. Sprinkle flour, stir well and pour in the scallop juice kept from the cooking operation. Then add the cream and whisk sauce gently. Simmer for 10 minutes, season and add lemon juice. Gently stir in half the grated cheese.
8 Pour sauce over scallops in shells. Sprinkle the rest of the grated cheese. Brown under the grill before serving.

Variations

A Omit mushrooms and onions from sauce, and just make a plain cheese sauce.
B As scallops are fairly expensive, mix in an equal quantity of ordinary white fish with the scallops. Poach for 5 minutes with the scallops.
C Add a few shrimps or prawns to the basic recipe, and a pinch of fresh herbs.

Chef's Tips

- make sure you keep the scallop shells — they can be used time and time again. Use fresh or frozen scallops.
- to produce a smooth mashed potato that's easy to pipe, allow 1 egg yolk and 1oz/25g butter per pound of potato.
- if you can't get the fishmonger to open scallops for you this is how to do it: place them on the top of a stove on a tray and heat gently. They will open Or use an oyster knife.

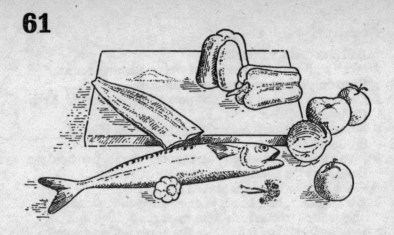

61

Sea-Food Creole

A rich sea-food casserole with onions, peppers and tomatoes

Ingredients

fish fillets (2 lbs/900g) cut in small pieces: use red mullet, bream, herring, mackerel, haddock or cod
oil (3fl oz/75ml)
onions (5oz/150g) chopped
garlic 2 cloves chopped
green peppers (4oz/100g) chopped
red pepper (2oz/50g) seeded and chopped

tomatoes (1 lb/450g) skinned, seeded and chopped
salt and **pepper** to taste
chilli powder a pinch
parsley and **oregano** 1 Tbs each chopped
seasoned flour (2oz/50g)

Preparation time 15 mins   **Cooking time** 25 mins
Portions 8   **Calories per portion** 250

Method

1 Clean, wash, skin and cut the fish into small pieces.
2 Drain and pass in seasoned flour.

3 Heat oil and sauté onions and peppers for 8 mins. Cover while doing so, then add garlic and fish, and place tomato pieces on top.
4 Season then cover with a lid and simmer for a further 10 minutes.
5 Sprinkle on chopped parsley and serve with boiled rice.

Variations

A Pass the fish in seasoned flour. Dip in oil and place in a shallow dish. Top up with all the other ingredients and seasoning. Bake in the oven for 20 minutes at 180 °C/ 350 °F/Gas Mark 4, covered with a lid.
B Omit the rice if the fish is served cold. Just add 3 Tbs vinegar or equivalent of lemon or lime juice. Serve with lettuce leaves.
C The fish can be pan-fried and served on the bone. In this case pour garnish and sauce over the fish.

Chef's Tips

- a more oriental flavour can be produced by adding a pinch of curry powder, or some soya sauce, or pineapple juice (or combination of these).
- or try sprinkling on fresh herbs before serving (tarragon, parsley and mint).
- blend in 1 Tbs mango chutney or any sweet pickle of your choice.

INDEX